FEDERAL NARCOTICS ENFORCEMENT

FEDERAL NARCOTICS ENFORCEMENT

Reorganization and Reform

PATRICIA RACHAL
Queens College
of the City University of New York

 Auburn House Publishing Company
Boston, Massachusetts

Library of Congress Cataloging in Publication Data

Rachal, Patricia, 1952–
  Federal narcotics enforcement.

  Includes index.
  1. Narcotics, Control of—United States—Management. 2. United States—Executive departments—Management. I. Title.
HV5825.R32   353.0076′5   82–1722
ISBN 0–86569–089–8   AACR2

Printed in the United States of America

*To my parents, Pearl and Charles Hill
and John Rachal,
for their love and understanding*

PREFACE

Reorganization of the federal government is a perennial and controversial issue—perennial because presidents find its potential alluring, both as a management tool and a political tool, and controversial because congressional committees, relevant clientele groups, and affected agencies may find it threatening to their interests. Despite their frequent use, experience suggests that reorganizations rarely fulfill the expectations of their architects; more often they result in disillusionment and failure.

The purpose of this study is to examine why reorganizations fail more often than they succeed. There are many accounts of reorganization failures. What makes this study different is that it goes beyond an analysis of the politics and process of reorganization and examines the consequences. It focuses on the reasons why calls for reorganization are so often repeated, the common obstacles standing in the path of successful reorganization, and those factors inherent in reorganization plans that generally doom them to failure.

Chapters 1 through 4 address the questions of why presidents so willingly embrace reorganization as a welcome panacea for a variety of organizational and political ills, and why Congress, interest groups, and federal agencies are so loath to view reorganization with the same enthusiasm.

Chapters 5 through 10 offer an in-depth empirical analysis of one federal reorganization—the Nixon Administration's 1973 attempt to reorganize federal narcotics law enforcement activities (Reorganization Plan No. 2 of 1973). This detailed case study into how and why the reorganization was proposed and an examination of its consequences is included in order to begin to fill the void in the empirical literature on federal reorganization and to provide an empirical basis on which to build more theoretical explanations for the frequent failure of reorganizations to have a real impact on the activities of federal agencies. If reorganizations are to be used with periodic frequency (and there is little reason to believe otherwise), then we need to develop reasonable expectations about what reorganizations can and cannot accomplish. This book attempts to move us in the direction of a more realistic assessment of the potential benefits and costs of reorganization by coupling theoretical understandings of reorganization with empirical work.

PAT RACHAL

ACKNOWLEDGMENTS

It was Sandy Maisel of Colby College who first got me interested in the study of political science, who first taught me how exciting and stimulating a discipline it could be. I thank him for that.

I am particularly indebted to Professor James Q. Wilson of Harvard University. I highly value the intellectual and moral support, the encouragement and wise counsel, he has given me over the years. I also gratefully acknowledge the research funds I received from the Alfred P. Sloan Foundation in support of the study of public management, and Professor Wilson's assistance in acquiring such.

To those at Auburn House, most notably John Harney and Gene Bailey, whose editorial advice, encouragement, and good cheer were most appreciated, I extend my thanks.

Finally, I would like to pay special thanks to a close friend and colleague, John T. Tierney, of Georgetown University. Without his assistance in a variety of tasks and without his steadfast flow of moral support, this book would never have been written. The gratitude I express here cannot possibly convey the depth of my appreciation for all his efforts.

P.R.

CONTENTS

FEDERAL NARCOTICS ENFORCEMENT

Chapter 1

INTRODUCTION

> *We trained hard . . . but it seemed that every time*
> *we were beginning to form up into teams we would*
> *be reorganized. I was to learn later in life that we*
> *tend to meet any new situation by reorganizing; and*
> *a wonderful method it can be for creating the illu-*
> *sion of progress while producing confusion, ineffi-*
> *ciency, and demoralization.*
>
> PETRONIUS ARBITER
> First Century, A.D.

If anything is constant about the structure of the federal government, it is change. Federal reorganization is one method through
which change, in the name of a wide variety of objectives, is
sought. The promise to reorganize the bureaucracy has long been
a rallying cry of presidential candidates and political executives
of all stripes. For example, when Jimmy Carter ran for president
in 1976, he called the executive branch a "horrible, bloated mess."
He promised to reorganize the bureaucracy into a sleeker, better
tuned machine that would be more efficient, effective, and responsive to the people. But Carter's vision of a reorganized
bureaucracy, like the visions of many of those who tried before
him, was clouded by failures.

Indeed, experience suggests that it is the rare reorganization
that fulfills its expectations or that has a substantial impact on the
output of the affected agencies—that is, on the delivery of public
services. Yet, despite the consistent failures and the resultant dis-
illusionments, reorganization remains an alluring instrument for
new administrations. Presidents are attracted to reorganization
for a variety of reasons, not the least of which is that it offers a
readily available and visible means of fulfilling, or attempting to
fulfill, campaign promises to whip into shape a flabby and unresponsive government.

1

Why Reorganize?

Reorganization, from the perspective of the White House, holds value both as a management tool and as a political tool. As a result, the reasons for proposing reorganizations may run the gamut from serious organizational attempts at improving the government's performance in a particular policy arena to reasons tied more closely to a desire to achieve some tactical political advantage. For example, presidents have often issued calls for reorganization specifically to address what they view as debilitating organizational problems or deficiencies. Reorganizations in this instance have serious, substantive goals linked to improved delivery of governmental services. Such presidents have sought to consolidate program responsibilities strewn throughout a large number of federal agencies to improve coordination and reduce confusion. Or they have sought to reduce overlaps in the jurisdictions and authority of two or more agencies—a policy deemed consistent with the norms of "good management."

In fact, presidential reliance on the "proverbs of organization" (for example, eliminate overlap and duplication, promote economy and efficiency, consolidate similar functions, and so forth) when advancing reorganization proposals is, of course, established practice. Indeed, Congress mandates their application to justify proposals submitted under the president's reorganization plan authority. But such rationales or justifications, while perhaps one factor in seeking a restructuring, are not always the most important or relevant explanations for reorganizing. As any astute observer of the federal bureaucracy knows, organizational structure carries political significance as well. Harold Seidman notes:[1]

> *Organizational arrangements are not neutral. We do not organize in a vacuum. Organization is one way of expressing national commitment, influencing program direction, and ordering priorities. Organizational arrangements tend to give some interests and perspectives more effective access to those with decision-making authority, whether they be in the Congress or in the executive branch.*

Hence, proposed alterations in agency structure or program alignment may be indicative more of a desire to affect the allocation of political power and authority than of a desire to improve the efficiency and effectiveness of the units involved. For example, the location of a particular program within the federal bureaucracy may be valued simply because of the visibility and access such a location accords that program. Using reorganization to change that spot on the organizational chart may serve effective symbolic notice of the administration's desire to lower that program's status or priority.

Changes in policy emphasis may be achieved through strategic reorganization as well. Moving a program into another agency or department may alter the program's focus or impact if only because the new agency embraces different procedures in carrying out its tasks. The application of these new procedures to the transferred program's activities may well result in a changed emphasis and thus a different output.

Reorganizations, too, may be used as a means of moving certain public officials into or out of power. For example, an official who has fallen into disfavor with the ruling administration may be ousted or demoted as a consequence of restructuring the agency's authority or jurisdiction. Removing certain responsibilities from individuals, or "kicking them upstairs" through reorganization, is one way to avoid unpleasant confrontations and charges of political expediency that a more public firing or request for resignation might entail.

Some reorganizations, of course, are nothing more than a logical response to routine, noncontroversial, operational problems that carry no political overtones. Reorganization may be the most likely and useful reaction to such problems as an increase in an agency's work load, changes in an organization's technology, or the large addition of new personnel to an existing organization.[2]

Whether reorganization is resorted to by presidents for the purpose of providing symbolic responses to calls for action or extracting some tactical political advantage or achieving serious, substantive improvements in the functioning of the federal government is an important issue. If we are to enhance our understanding of why presidential restructurings so often are considered failures, sorting the reasons for reorganization into meaningful categories is critical. For example, a reorganization might have failed to achieve its stated goal of increasing an organization's efficiency and effectiveness, yet perhaps succeeded in achieving an important, but unstated, goal of punishing an official or lowering the status of the agency or program in question. The statutory need for presidents to defend or justify reorganizations based on the traditional proverbs of organization, combined with the use of this orthodoxy to mask the more political goals of reorganization, transforms a seemingly easy task—categorizing the goals of reorganization—into a more nettlesome one. Only by examining and analyzing reorganization "failures" in terms of their true objectives can we begin to think of ways to devise more successful reorganizations.

Those who have studied and written about federal reorganizations have gathered a long list of objectives that reorganizers purport to seek.[3] But developing a useful typology of reorganization goals has not been as widely attempted.

Lester Salamon is one who has given careful thought to this need for developing a framework for thinking about the goals of reorganization. He suggests three general categories into which the goals may be sorted: (1) economy and efficiency, (2) policy effectiveness, and (3) tactical political advantage.[4] Obviously, reorganizations may serve two or more objectives at once. And, as Salamon suggests, one must be wary of succumbing to a "false dichotomy" between the political and substantive goals of reorganization.[5]

Nevertheless, while recognizing the need to stay alert to Salamon's warning, the purpose here is to ask why it is that those reorganizations that seek to achieve serious, substantive change so often fail to deliver the promised benefits. Although such reorganizations may carry ancillary, political goals, their primary purpose is to improve the government's performance in a given policy arena. Reorganizations may be defended in terms of economy or efficiency, or they may be interpreted as seeking some political advantage for the president. Many reorganizations, however, if not most, are aimed at the more serious goal of positively affecting the outcomes of federal policies.[6]

Resistance to Reorganization

Whatever the goals of reorganization, stated or unstated, the nature of our political system almost ensures the arousal of an opposition, except in the most innocuous of cases. Included among the traditional opponents of change are congressional committees, federal agencies, and the relevant outside interest groups.

Reorganization as viewed from Congress may pose threats to members whose committee jurisdictions might be affected by a restructuring. For example, reorganization may threaten the existence of political subsystems (composed of congressional committees, federal agencies, and interest groups), a relationship closely guarded by those involved. The goals of reorganization, therefore, may be of little importance to congressional members intent on protecting their spheres of authority and influence. A presidential reorganization that threatens to upset the congressional committee structure, no matter how rational and reasonable, surely will irk those who might be adversely affected by the restructuring.

Agencies, too, are another natural opponent to executive reorganization. Their objections may range from personnel fears of a loss in rank or civil service status, to concerns over a change in a valued agency ethos or mission, to a shared concern with Congress over the breaking apart of a mutually beneficial subsystem.

Clientele groups also may find reorganization distasteful, especially if it imperils ties to contacts and allies within the organizations to be affected. Interest groups over time become comfortable with an agency's methods of operation and become protective of their access to key decisionmakers in agencies with which they have frequent communication. Change breeds uncertainty and jeopardizes established ways of doing business. For this reason alone reorganization may be opposed, despite any claims of new benefits to be gained.

Presidents, of course, may choose to reorganize precisely because they wish to disrupt the cozy relationships that can arise between these three common sources of opposition to bureaucratic realignment. However, as Chapters 3 and 4 illustrate, any one of these three interests can present formidable stumbling blocks to presidential reorganizations—regardless of whether those reorganizations are serious attempts at improving government performance or efforts aimed at achieving some kind of tactical political advantage.

Understanding the Failures

Even if presidents are successful in deflecting the usual opponents of reorganization or in assuaging their fears of change, it might be of small consolation in the end. Federal reorganizations, it seems, rarely produce the results touted and promised by their architects. There are many accounts of reorganization efforts and there are many who assert that reorganizations fail more often than they succeed. The purpose of this study is to explain why. What makes this study different from others is that it goes beyond an analysis of the politics and process of reorganization and examines its consequences. It suggests reasons why there are recurrent calls for reorganization, what traditional obstacles to reorganization stand in the path of presidents bent on reorganizing, and, most importantly, what it is about reorganization proposals that generally dooms them to failure. Only by understanding both the process and *outcomes* of reorganization can we gain greater insight into how reorganization can be used more successfully as a management tool.

Scholars and practitioners of public administration alike have long lamented the dearth of empirical cases dealing with the creation and implementation of reorganizations. The lack of research into what reorganizations accomplish—or fail to accomplish—is a theme repeatedly articulated by some of the most noted observers of federal reorganization efforts. For example, Frederick Mosher has commented that empirical studies of reorganization are "few and thin" and offer little insight into the actual effects of reorganizations on the operations of the affected agencies.[7] Harold Seidman has observed that although we often seem to expect reorganizations to produce "miracles," there exists "almost no systematic analysis to determine what in fact reorganizations achieve."[8] And Lester Salamon has labeled our knowledge about the matter "woefully inadequate," with serious empirical work on reorganization not just deficient, but close to nonexistent.[9]

The dearth of empirical work is not surprising. After all, quality case studies require tremendous investments of time and resources. Moreover, case studies in general enjoy little currency in certain political science circles, where they are viewed as methodologically deficient and intellectually suspect. These are empty arguments, however. The only way to test theories (and one good way to promulgate new ones) on why reorganizations are proposed and why they so often fail is to produce a body of empirical evidence on which generalizations can be based.

This book begins to fill the empirical void in our knowledge of why and how reorganizations are proposed and to what effect. It does so, first, by reviewing the reasons why presidents seek to reorganize and what obstacles are likely to thwart reorganization attempts, and second, by presenting and analyzing in detail the Nixon Administration's 1973 reorganization of federal narcotics law enforcement activities. Reorganization Plan No. 2 of 1973 was chosen as the focus of an in-depth examination of a presidential reorganization attempt because it represented a serious, well-intentioned effort to change the way federal narcotics agencies were performing public functions. The reorganization plan was designed to consolidate federal narcotics law enforcement activities into one lead agency, the Drug Enforcement Administration (DEA), in the Justice Department. The expectation was that a new alignment of agencies and jurisdictions would end vexing bureaucratic rivalries and significantly upgrade the effectiveness of the federal government's drug enforcement program. Important presidential political stakes were involved as well: the narcotics law enforcement effort was linked directly to Richard Nixon's "war on heroin," to which the president had accorded high priority. A detailed investigation into how and why this reorganization was proposed and a review of its consequences (Chapters 5 through 9) provide an empirical underpinning on which to base more theoretical explanations for the frequent failure of reorganizations to make any real difference in the outcomes of federal agencies. For example, this case suggests that the nature of the analysis preceding the drafting of reorganizations must be altered if reorganizations are to be devised in such a way that they will have a significant impact on the activities of the federal government. Yet, as the case of Reorganization Plan No. 2 of 1973 shows, serious cognitive and political constraints tend to impede both the development and implementation of a reorganization motivated by a serious, substantive goal.

The Costs of Reorganizing

Although little empirical evidence currently exists to instruct us on what reorganizations can and do achieve, we do know that the costs of reorganization are often high. For example, for the president the costs may involve a large expenditure of expensive political capital with offsetting gains far from assured. For an agency the costs may range from lowered morale to negative effects on the organization's sense of mission and ethos. For Congress, the potential costs include unwelcome alterations of committee jurisdictions or the disruption of important policy subsystems. Even the public may suffer by having to shoulder the costs of program interruption or disarray.

Indeed, the costs of reorganization are potentially so great and so disruptive that as a management tool the use of this device may in fact be dysfunctional. Bureaucratic organization is supposed to make government behavior calculable and predictable; constant reorganization makes both less likely. Repeated reorganizations, whatever their rationale, are very disruptive, if not harmful, to the pursuit of program goals. Thus, a careful weighing of the costs of reorganization versus the potential gains is of great importance if reorganization is to avoid dysfunctional effects.

Nevertheless, it is safe to assume that presidents and other political executives will continue to embrace reorganization as a panacea for a variety of organizational, operational, and political ills. If for this reason only, then, the study of reorganization is important. As long as the tool of reorganization continues to be used with periodic frequency in attempts to bring about substantive change, there exists a need to better our understanding of the process of reorganization and of what results can logically be attained. For reorganization to be a valuable device, we need to set realistic expectations about what reorganization can and cannot do. Lowered expectations and more reasonable and accurate rationales accompanying reorganization proposals may, for example, help to minimize implementation problems and avoid unanticipated and unintended consequences of reorganization.

Developing reasonable expectations, however, requires a close examination of past attempts at reorganization to determine if the consequences of a change were the ones intended and, if not, why not. Only then will we be in a position to devise reorganizations with realistic assessments of their potential costs and realistic expectations of their potential benefits. To that end, more empirical work is essential and should prove instructive. This book is a step in that direction.

Endnotes

1. Harold Seidman, *Politics, Position, and Power*, 3d ed. (New York: Oxford University Press, 1980), p. 15.
2. James W. Davis, Jr., *An Introduction to Public Administration* (New York: The Free Press, 1974), pp. 292–93.
3. Lester M. Salamon, "The Goals of Reorganization," *Administration and Society* 12 (February 1981):478.
4. *Ibid.*, p. 479.
5. *Ibid.*, p. 472.
6. *Ibid.*, p. 485.
7. Frederick C. Mosher, "Some Notes on Reorganizations in Public Agencies," in Roscoe C. Martin, ed., *Public Administration and Democracy* (Syracuse, N.Y.: Syracuse University Press, 1965), pp. 130–31.
8. Remarks by Harold Seidman in Douglas M. Fox, ed., "A Mini-Symposium, President Nixon's Proposals for Executive Reorganization," *Public Administration Review* 34 (September/October 1974):489.
9. Salamon, "The Goals of Reorganization," p. 474.

Chapter 2

REORGANIZATION: THE PRESIDENTIAL PERSPECTIVE

Administrative management of the federal bureaucratic machinery has long been an issue of major concern for presidents and top executives of all political persuasions. Since the emergence of the "administrative state"[1] (referring to the multitude of governmental units and the number of officials who staff these organizations), control and coordination of the federal bureaucracy has presented a formidable challenge to those charged with the task.

Presidential Powers over the Bureaucracy

The Constitution makes no mention of an executive bureaucracy. Hence, control over the administrative apparatus has been the source of some friction and much debate between members of the legislative branch and occupants of the White House. Certainly, the Founding Fathers never envisioned a federal bureaucracy of today's size and scope. As a result, the Constitution makes little provision for and offers little guidance as to how the powers and authority over the executive machinery should be divided or shared. Yet the Founding Fathers clearly were intent on correcting the administrative chaos that had reigned under the Articles of Confederation when management rested in the hands of the Continental Congress. Additionally, the Constitution does instruct the president to take care that "the Laws be faithfully executed." The role of the president as chief executive officer is viewed as having its roots in that phrase. Congress, of course, does hold considerable powers and prerogatives when it comes to overseeing the administrative system. For example, Congress can create and abolish federal agencies and departments, appropriate funds for agency operations, and pass legislation affecting the details of agency activities. More recently, Congress has made increasingly frequent use of the legislative veto to influence the nature of rules and regulations promulgated by agencies.

Most would agree, however, that the president is the one who stands as titular head of the federal bureaucracy. The problem of managing—controlling and coordinating—the bureaucratic machinery, then, is a burden that Congress partially shares, but one that rests largely on the shoulders of the president. As the bureaucracy has grown in size and as its discretionary power has expanded, Congress has consented to delegate to the president substantial powers aimed at strengthening the president's managerial hand. For example, Congress has (1) authorized the president to create an EOP (Executive Office of the President) to provide assistants and advisors for administrative matters, (2) accorded the president much discretion in appointing officials to top-level policy-making positions within the bureaucracy, (3) added to the president's budgetary powers, and (4) allowed the president to reorganize the executive branch structure subject to congressional approval.[2] Congress has granted the president these powers in part because it recognizes the difficulty in checking a bureaucracy that has considerable latitude in carrying out its activities.

A brief review of presidential powers that can be exercised to enhance control over the administrative system may at first glance appear impressive. After all, the president has significant powers in the following areas:[3]

1. The power of appointment, affording the president the opportunity through careful and deliberate personnel choices to influence policy direction and agency behavior.
2. Substantial budgetary authority, allowing the president through the actions of OMB and use of White House legislative clearance procedures to mold agency requests for funds and new legislation for presidential program priorities.
3. Authority extrapolated from the president's power as commander-in-chief and generalized to the domestic sphere to reverse administrative decisions made by agencies.

4. The right, delegated by Congress, to alter the organizational structure of agencies, through which the president can affect their location, status, priorities, and jurisdiction.

Limits on Presidential Control

Yet, despite these broad authorities and powers, presidential control of the federal bureaucracy does not come easily. Indeed, most recent presidents, while articulating their desire to "cure the ills of big government," have soon become disillusioned with the prospects of finding a quick and easy remedy for bureaucratic problems. The frustration felt by many presidents over their seeming inability to coordinate and check the activities of the bureaucracy are reflected in Franklin Roosevelt's description of his dealings with the bureaucratic machinery:[4]

> *The Treasury is so large and far-flung and ingrained in its practices that I find it almost impossible to get the actions and results I want—even with Henry [Morgenthau] there. But the Treasury is not to be compared with the State Department. You should go through the experience of trying to get changes in the thinking, policy, and action of the career diplomats and then you'd know what a real problem was. But the Treasury and the State Department put together are nothing compared with the Na-a-vy. The admirals are really something to cope with—and I should know. To change anything in the Na-a-vy is like punching a feather bed. You punch it with your right and you punch it with your left until you are finally exhausted, and then you find the damn bed just as it was before you started punching.*

Indeed, most of Roosevelt's successors have encountered similar frustrations in attempting to bring order and coherence to the federal bureaucracy. John F. Kennedy became so dismayed with his own dealings with the State Department that he referred to it as a "bowl of jelly." Richard Nixon repeatedly lamented his inability to instill any "discipline" or "loyalty" in those working for him in the federal bureaucracy. And Jimmy Carter's view of a bureaucracy unresponsive to the people (and to the president) was confirmed by a seemingly trivial incident—he once found himself cornered in the Oval Office by a dead mouse and two feuding bureaucracies, the General Services Administration and the Department of the Interior, neither of which would remove the decaying carcass, claiming it fell under the other's jurisdiction.

Presidents' attempts to control the federal bureaucracy are thwarted in part because of certain limitations on the exercise of their powers—limitations that tend to dilute their potential managerial influence. One constraint is time. No modern president has the time necessary for detailed supervision of bureaucratic operations. Even with the massive growth of the presidential advisory system, following up on presidential instructions to agencies is impossible—except in those instances where vigorous White House oversight is considered crucial because of the priority attached to a presidential decision. Even direct and explicit presidential orders are resisted by career bureaucrats who choose to ignore, delay, or otherwise subvert clear instructions in the absence of White House oversight. For example, although Richard Nixon instructed officials in the Department of Health, Education, and Welfare to relax pressures on schools to desegregate, HEW personnel continued to pursue policies in direct opposition to the president's orders.[5]

Another constraint related to that of time is the inadequacy of the information available to a president to ensure close control of the bureaucracy—such information is often insufficient or overwhelming. The sheer number of executive bureaucracies that the president must oversee and the vast amount of output they generate mean that a president must make judicious decisions about where to focus his efforts and which agencies must be scrutinized closely. Again, presidential priorities and interests will dictate where this attention will fall and what information will be used or sought to regulate agency behavior. Thus, many agencies will escape a detailed review by the White House staff because of time and information constraints. Only those agencies engaged in work of great interest and importance to the president or agencies that are involved in a crisis, scandal, or publicized mismanagement of agency activities receive direct presidential attention.

Finally, a president's efforts to control the bureaucracy may be hindered because of having to share authority with the legislative branch. For example, Congress may not always agree with presidential initiatives or policy emphases and may pressure agency administrators into a change of course. Congress may also disagree with the budget recommendations made by a president, choosing instead to increase or decrease the level of funding for a particular agency or program. Governmental subsystems, too, can effectively thwart attempts by the president to make an imprint on bureaucratic operations. These subsystems, consisting of federal agencies, congressional committees, and special interests, can present a formidable obstacle to presidents intent on exercising their powers to affect agency behavior or to alter the existing alignment of federal units. The elements of these subsystems will marshal their resources to impede such presidential actions if they are viewed as threatening. Congressional committees are often suspicious of presidential reorganization proposals, regardless of the existence of governmental subsystems, because they fear a loss of power or a cutting back of committee jurisdiction.

Some students of the presidency have suggested that these constraints on the exercise of presidential powers are not the only factors limiting a president's influence over the bureaucracy. They argue that the administrative woes of a president may be related as well to the background and training of recent occupants of the White House. For example, many presidents have prepared for the nation's highest post by serving in Congress—as did Harry Truman, John Kennedy, Lyndon Johnson, Richard Nixon, and Gerald Ford. While in many ways providing excellent training for the nation's top office, Congress does not, however, prepare a president for the vast managerial responsibilities that are assumed upon taking office. To be sure, members of Congress have much contact with the bureaucracy, but the nature of that contact is, as Kenneth Meier has noted, "more cooperative than hierarchical."[6] The congressional committee system and the obligatory constituent work all members must engage in do provide regular opportunities for legislators to interact with federal agencies. But the specialized nature of this work does not provide legislators with a comprehensive overview of the bureaucracy nor does it hone broader managerial skills. Even those presidents who have boasted of their administrative experience, as did Jimmy Carter, have encountered more frustration than satisfaction when trying to apply their talents to the federal administrative machinery. Relying on the appointment process to place experienced managers throughout the executive branch is not much help either— consider the fact that Carter had the opportunity to fill fewer than one hundred positions in the Treasury Department, amounting to less than 1 per cent of that department's total work force.[7]

Reorganization as a Management Tool

Despite the array of tools at the president's disposal, control of
the federal bureaucracy remains an elusive goal. Nonetheless,
presidents and their top political appointees feel obligated, once
in office, to grapple with the "bureaucracy problem" they so often
attacked with campaign rhetoric. One of the most consistently
employed methods in pursuit of a more rational and responsive
bureaucracy is executive reorganization.

Reorganization as a tool of presidential management is ap-
pealing for a number of reasons. Certainly it provides a highly
visible means of illustrating to the public the president's intent
to keep campaign promises. Indeed, a favorite tactic of political
executives is to announce major reorganization goals immediately
upon taking office. Jimmy Carter, for example, began his tenure
as president by creating a reorganization unit in OMB that was
charged with preparing plans to reduce 1,900 federal agencies
down to a more manageable 200. Intradepartmental reorganization is often one of the first publicly announced decisions of
executives who have been chosen by a new president to run
large federal bureaucracies. For example, Robert Nimmo, Ronald
Reagan's choice to head the Veterans' Administration, took little
time in confirming his intent to realign the VA staff; Anne M.
Gorsuch, another Reagan appointee, announced a major reorganization of the Environmental Protection Agency not long after
taking office; and Norman Bradman, rumored to be President
Reagan's selection to head the Immigration and Naturalization
Service, did not even wait for confirmation of his nomination before stating that one of his first acts would be to implement a
radical reorganization of the problem-plagued INS. Even those
officials who recognize the traumas and costs of repeated reorganization and its potentially adverse, if not dysfunctional, effects
on agency morale and operations may still opt to reorganize, as
did the incoming commissioner of the Social Security Administration in 1979. Stanford G. Ross defended his actions by noting:[8]

> *As I began my evaluation, I quickly sensed that SSA had not fully*
> *recovered from the organizational trauma of the 1975 reorganiza-*
> *tion and that there appeared to be a rather deep-seated fear of*
> *organizational change on the part of many of SSA's staff. . . .*
> *However, . . . our current organizational structure hampers ef-*

*fective and meaningful communications, inhibits the policy de-
velopment and decision-making process, contains duplication, and
isolates the field organization to the extent that field interests and
concerns are not adequately represented at headquarters. The
magnitude and diversity of these problems demand organizational change if SSA is to effectively perform its mission.*

Significant structural changes aimed at improving the performance of the federal government are generally couched in
language related to the principles or proverbs of "good management." These organizational principles, as applied to government
reorganization, have their roots in the work of the Brownlow Committee in the 1930s and in the work of the First Hoover Commission in the late 1940s. The Reorganization Act of 1949, which
delegates reorganization authority to the president, lists many of
these principles as the proper justification for executive reorganizations. They include (1) promotion of efficiency and economy in government operations, (2) reduction of overlap, duplication, and waste, (3) consolidation of similar functions, (4)
abolishment of unnecessary functions, and (5) grouping of organizational functions according to major purposes.[9]

The expressed goals of reorganizations devised today are still
tied to these organizational principles, despite the criticism that
these nostrums are inadequate for, or irrelevant to, current administrative problems or the use of reorganization as a presidential
control device. Although dissatisfaction with these orthodoxies
goes back at least to Franklin Roosevelt (he argued, for example,
that the notion of tying reorganization to the objective of economy was wrong because it had little to do with good management), presidents have continued to rely on these principles as
justification for reorganizing. This is due, in part, to congressional
insistence on receiving presidential reorganization proposals with
rationales based on the classical theories of organization. Harold
Seidman is just one of many who are troubled by the need to
follow this "prescribed ritual":[10]

*Necessary though it may have been to establish a legal founda-
tion for an extraordinary grant of powers to the president, the
long-run effects of freezing the purposes and principles of organization into law have been most unfortunate. They have inhibited
creative thinking about federal structure and the development of
fresh approaches adapted to the needs of our times. They have
sometimes provided the right answers, but often for the wrong
reasons.*

Yet even Carter's reorganization group felt it was necessary to come up with assessments of the potential savings to be reaped through reorganization. One Carter White House aide commented that it was his desire to devise an economic development and natural resource reorganization plan that could be advanced with a promise of saving "many millions of dollars," in hopes of drumming up additional congressional support for the measure.[11]

Reliance on the orthodox theory to justify reorganization can hamper presidents who wish to use reorganization as a tool of management control, by forcing them to tailor their reorganization proposals to the prescribed principles. Of course, many reorganizations are serious and substantive efforts to solve vexing bureaucratic problems. In such cases, forwarding a presidential message to Congress explaining the reorganization in terms of the established principles poses few problems. For example, the 1973 reorganization of narcotics law enforcement jurisdictions was aimed at resolving long-standing and bitter disputes between federal agencies with overlapping responsibilities, and President Nixon's message to Congress indicated just that.

In seeking control over the bureaucratic machinery, however, presidents may resort to reorganization for purposes that are not directly or clearly related to improvements in the delivery of governmental services. In these instances reorganization may be used to achieve some tactical political advantage or to redirect policy emphasis. Yet even reorganizations of this sort will be justified by reference to the objectives set forth in the Reorganization Act of 1949, thus masking the true goals of reorganization. The real objectives can range from the desire to increase or lower the visibility or power of specific agencies or specific officials, to a desire to break up established subsystems or bureaucratic fiefdoms. And, of course, reorganization can represent nothing more than a symbolic gesture aimed at placating a disgruntled constituency or employed to offer a tangible response to a complex or especially troubling bureaucratic problem that is unrelated to organizational structure. Large-scale reorganizations, such as the one proposed by Richard Nixon in 1970 to revamp totally the number and alignment of cabinet-level departments, may be advanced with familiar justifications—to streamline, consolidate, or in some way make more rational the organization of the federal government. Even in these cases, however, reorganization may be perceived by some as harboring more political goals—such as a president's desire to gain more political influence over an entrenched bureaucracy that is viewed as being hostile to presidential goals and priorities.

The Sources of Reorganization Proposals

Presidents can delegate responsibility for devising reorganization proposals to a variety of different groups. National commissions are generally used by presidents when an overarching reorganization is sought—one that seeks to achieve wholesale, across-the-board changes in the alignment of federal organizations. The Brownlow Committee (officially known as the President's Committee on Administrative Management), the two Hoover Commissions on the Organization of the Executive Branch of the Government, and the Advisory Council on Executive Organization, headed by Roy Ash, are examples of units created specifically to address the issue of executive reorganization. Each had a relatively broad mandate to study the government's organizational structure and to submit recommendations for how administrative management of the federal bureaucracy could be improved.

The use of task forces to help with the creation of reorganization plans is another method favored by presidents, and one popularized by Presidents Kennedy and Johnson. These are usually ad hoc groups whose membership may include members of the White House staff, top executives of the agencies or departments to be affected, OMB officials, and perhaps one or two career-level bureaucrats whose organizations are to be studied. Reorganization task forces usually have a short life span and a narrower focus than do national commissions.

Congressional committees may be requested by a president to review the prospects for reorganization in a particular area, or they may of their own volition undertake an investigation with the intent of proposing a reorganization. And, of course, congressional committees always have the opportunity to review reorganization proposals created by the president under the authority of the Reorganization Act of 1949.

Finally, private organizations may also be a source of reorganization proposals, engaging in their work sometimes at the request of a president and sometimes acting on their own initiative. For example, the National Academy of Public Administration prepared a report on its own initiative in 1974, issued in the wake of the Watergate crisis, recommending many organizational changes in the executive branch.[12]

Whatever the source of reorganization proposals (task forces today being the most common), the nature of analysis relied on by those charged with creating reorganizations rarely involves in-depth or field examinations of the organizational units to be affected. In fact, the primary guides to what form a reorganization should take are the conventional wisdoms, the general administrative experience of those serving on the task force or commission, and common sense.[13] It is unusual for a task force, for example, to conduct studies in the field, outside of Washington headquarters, to determine what kind of restructuring will have what effect on those operators who actually perform the tasks of the organization. Such analyses may not be of concern to those devising reorganizations aimed solely at achieving some tactical political advantage or even those directed at a change in policy emphasis. However, they are important and necessary if reorganizations are to be devised with a real chance of affecting or improving the delivery of important public services. But as the case of Reorganization Plan No. 2 of 1973 will show, generating useful data in a systematic way is difficult for reorganization planners to do, even when they have the best of intentions.

Summary

Executive reorganization and reforming the federal bureaucracy into a more responsive and accountable administrative system—in both a political and a managerial sense—are closely associated in the minds of presidents. Most modern presidents have utilized the tool of reorganization in search of an answer to the vexing "bureaucracy problem." And most who have tried it have been disappointed in the results. Executive reorganization requires a great commitment of presidential resources and large expenditures of a president's political capital. The obstacles that lay in the path of a president bent on reorganizing the federal government can be most formidable, however, as the following two chapters show.

A president must decide, then, if any reorganization is worth the costs, often high, that accompany the struggle for congressional acceptance—especially when past experience suggests that the eventual results of reorganization will often fall short of those promised by its architects.

Nevertheless, despite the risks involved, and despite the powerful forces that stand ready to resist proposals viewed as threatening to their interests, reorganization remains in attractive tool for presidents determined to enhance their control over the administrative network they head.

Endnotes

1. For a historical review of the factors leading to the rise of the administrative state, see, for example, James Q. Wilson, "The Rise of the Bureaucratic State," in Francis E. Rourke, ed., *Bureaucratic Power in National Politics* (Boston: Little, Brown & Co., 1978), pp. 54–78.
2. Lawrence C. Dodd and Richard L. Schott, *Congress and the Administrative State* (New York: John Wiley & Sons, 1979), pp. 3–4.
3. Kenneth J. Meier, *Politics and the Bureaucracy* (No. Scituate, Mass: Duxbury Press, 1979), pp. 146–51.
4. As quoted in Richard Neustadt, *Presidential Power* (New York: John Wiley & Sons, 1980), p. 33.
5. Meier, *Politics and the Bureaucracy*, p. 151. Richard Neustadt argues that obedience to presidential orders will occur only when certain conditions are met, ranging from the clarity of the order to bureaucrats' having the resources necessary to carry out the instructions. See Richard Neustadt, *Presidential Power*.
6. Meier, *Politics and the Bureaucracy*, p. 145.
7. James Q. Wilson, *American Government, Institutions, and Policies* (Lexington, Mass.: D. C. Heath and Co., 1980), p. 323.
8. As quoted in Laurence E. Lynn, Jr., *Managing the Public's Business* (New York: Basic Books, 1981), p. 86.
9. Harold Seidman, *Politics, Position, and Power* (New York: Oxford University Press, 1980), p. 10.
10. *Ibid.*, p. 10.
11. Lynn, *Managing the Public's Business*, p. 89.
12. Tyrus G. Fain, ed., *Federal Reorganization: The Executive Branch* (New York: R. R. Bowker Co., 1977), p. xxvi.
13. James W. Davis, Jr., *An Introduction to Public Administration* (New York: The Free Press, 1974), pp. 299–302.

Chapter 3

REORGANIZATION: THE CONGRESSIONAL PERSPECTIVE

Decisions about the structure and management of the federal executive branch are not the exclusive preserve of the president but are shared with Congress. Even though the president has considerable latitude in shaping the organization and direction of the federal executive branch, presidential preferences and choices are limited by Congress. Thus, in order to understand the organization of the executive branch—and to appreciate the problems involved in reorganizing it—it is necessary to understand the structure and dynamics of Congress and how the legislature shapes and delimits organizational decisions. As Harold Seidman has observed: "One could as well ignore the laws of aerodynamics in designing an aircraft as ignore the laws of congressional dynamics in designing executive branch structure."[1]

With respect to any given proposal for executive reorganization, there may be as many different views as there are members of Congress. After all, Congress is not a monolithic entity but an assembly of 535 individuals with different goals, interests, and concerns. Even so, one is on safe ground in arguing that the general reaction of members of Congress to proposed executive reorganizations will be shaped by the extent to which the reshuffling would disrupt the jurisdictions and powers of congressional committees.

Congressional Committees and "Subsystems"

The Constitution instructs each house of Congress to organize its internal proceedings as it sees fit. Both the Senate and the House have chosen to do so by creating a system of legislative committees to cope with their crowded agendas and heavy work loads. The organization of congressional committees and the division of responsibilities among them loosely parallel the jurisdictions and structure of the federal bureaucracy. And like the jurisdictions of federal agencies, congressional committee jurisdictions are often overlapping. As one observer has noted, "Existing [congressional committee] arrangements result from compromises and historical accidents, not from any conscious organizational philosophy or planning to achieve identified purposes."[2] Even so, it is within this system of standing committees and subcommittees that the real power of Congress lies and the real work of Congress takes place.

Each committee and subcommittee can best be understood as key components of what Douglass Cater first referred to as "subgovernments" or "subsystems."[3] These are relatively small groups or networks composed of the members (especially the senior members) of congressional committees or subcommittees, a few key bureaucrats from relevant agencies or bureaus, and interest group representatives, all of whom, by virtue of their regular interaction and shared information and expertise, make the important decisions in individual policy arenas. Only on highly visible and politically sensitive issues will the largely independent policymaking prerogatives of these subsystems be preempted by intervention on the part of the president or the whole House or Senate. Thus, the committees and subcommittees are important power bases for their members. They provide members with the opportunity to make substantive policy, help their constituents, build a national reputation, cultivate the support of outside clientele groups, and build strategic alliances with officials in the executive branch.

But the benefits of these subsystems are not all one-sided, enjoyed exclusively by the legislators. Rather, these are mutually supportive arrangements that naturally confer benefits on the executive agencies and the clientele groups as well. (For present purposes, we are interested primarily in the committees and the agencies.) The bureaucrats, after all, know that the support of Congress is highly contingent—that is (as James Q. Wilson has phrased it), "it may be withdrawn, altered, or reduced at any time, often without recourse or appeal (a bureau chief cannot sue a budget examiner or an appropriations committee chairman for breach of contract)."[4] Thus, it is in an agency's best interests to build personal and supportive relationships with members of those congressional committees that control the agency's statutory authority and the resources granted to it.

Although the cultivation of such relationships is easier in some instances than in others, most members of Congress are supportive and protective of the agencies within their jurisdiction. This tends to occur naturally by virtue of the regularized contact between committees and their bureaucratic charges. But there is more to it than that. Agencies will use every means at their disposal to curry the favor of relevant committee members, taking special care to provide services that cannot be found elsewhere. For example, an agency will be sure to handle any "constituency service" calls from a committee members' office with particular care and dispatch. More important, an agency will curry the support and goodwill of committee members by providing them with opportunities to claim credit for securing government benefits for their constituents, as when an agency lets a congressman announce the award of a community development block grant or a water resource project to his district (even when he may have had little or nothing to do with the decision). Of course, conversely, agencies may also go to pains to spare the districts of their committee allies from certain program cutbacks such as the closing of a military base or the elimination of a Public Health Service hospital, an Amtrak route, or a local post office.

Finally, agencies are in a position to provide committee members with the most precious resource in Washington political circles: information. Executive branch agencies are the repositories of vast amounts of expertise, technical information, and political intelligence that can be important assets to legislators interested in enhancing their reputation as policy experts or eager to improve their overall performance in committee proceedings.

In short, these subsystems are comfortable, mutually supportive networks that confer assorted benefits on the executive agencies,

congressional committee members, and clientele groups. Not surprisingly, committee members (and especially the chairmen and
others in positions of power) are eager to nurture and maintain
the organizational arrangements that sustain these subsystems.
They naturally want to maintain the existing organizational structure of the executive branch (and thus help to preserve the
existing jurisdictions of the standing congressional committees)
as a way of maintaining their personal decision-making prerogatives in key policy arenas, protecting the interests of others in the
subsystem, satisfying their own personal ambitions and power
drives, serving their reelection goals, and otherwise furthering
their careers.[5]

Conversely, an agency that is successful in building and nurturing a relationship with the appropriate members of Congress will
reap many benefits. In particular, such an agency may find itself
in a better position to deflect presidential reorganization plans—
especially those that would disrupt established networks or support systems.

Subsystem Allies:
An Obstacle to Reorganization

Subsystems tend to be viewed in somewhat less sanguine terms
by those who stand outside of them. Critics charge that these
"iron triangles" or "triple alliances" (as they have been variously
termed) make it difficult for other political actors to penetrate the
decision-making process in individual policy arenas. This is particularly troublesome, critics allege, because it discourages "breadth
of view" in the policymaking process, thus impeding a broader
definition of the public interest. This problem is presumably
further exacerbated if (as is alleged) congressional committees
eschew aggressive oversight of the agencies under their charge,
adopting more of a protective than an objective or critical relationship.

Even presidents often find their wishes and preferences
thwarted by the policy-specific subsystems. This is not surprising
since the agencies, congressional committees, and clientele groups
that constitute these policy networks are the repositories not only
of the best technical information and political intelligence con-

cerning a particular policy area, but of the strongest interests and fiercest commitments. Naturally, presidential reorganization proposals are among the most prominent threats to a subsystem's interests and are thus likely to meet staunch resistance.

Members of Congress, acting in concert with, or at the prodding of, other political actors, can present a formidable obstacle to presidential reorganization attempts. The legislators may want to protect their own personal power stakes inside the congressional committee system, or they may want to protect the policy goals or the interests of other elements of a subsystem. Whatever the reasons for their opposition, members of Congress have frequently frustrated presidents bent on reorganization.

For example, when President Lyndon Johnson reorganized federal transportation agencies in 1966, he was unable to convince Congress to include the Maritime Administration under the administrative umbrella of the new Department of Transportation, even though such a transfer was eminently logical. The Johnson Administration waged an extensive and strenuous legislative battle trying to include the Maritime Administration, but even the formidable political tacticians in the Johnson White House were unable to overcome the aroused opponents of the plan. A key to the Administration's defeat in this case was the extraordinary opposition generated by members of the House Maritime Committee, who were outraged over the prospect of forfeiting a major chunk of their jurisdiction as a result of the proposed reorganization. In a successful search for supporting votes among their House colleagues, Maritime Committee members relied on a revealing and potent argument: "If LBJ's transportation reorganization puts us out of business this year," they told their fellow representatives, "then he may send up another proposal which will put your favorite committee out of business next year."[6] Sympathetic (or perhaps alarmed) legislators responded in sufficient numbers to defeat the proposed transfer.

Concerns about the effects on congressional committee jurisdictions were also instrumental in defeating President Nixon's 1971 proposals to carry out a wholesale reorganization of the federal executive branch. Representative Chet Holifield, then chairman of the House Committee on Government Operations, told officials assembled at a hearing:[7]

If by this reorganization you affect in a major way the powers of the various committees in Congress, you may as well forget it. The only way I know to get one or more of these departments through is to allow the committees that now have the programs within their jurisdictions to follow these programs, just as they are followed now, and authorize these programs wherever they are distributed.

Several years later, the Carter Administration's push for creation of a new Department of Education set off another firestorm of controversies on Capitol Hill. Some members of the House seemed primarily concerned about the possibility that such a move might invite new efforts to split apart the House Education and Labor Committee. For example, in testimony before the House Government Operations Committee, Congresswoman Shirley Chisholm (D.–N.Y.) advised her colleagues:[8]

As Members of Congress, we must also take note of the impact the reorganization of HEW and federal education programs would probably have on the committee structure in the House of Representatives. Although my distinguished colleague, Chairman Perkins from the Education and Labor Committee, has denied the likelihood of committee division, others may decide to spearhead a drive to divide the committee.

But members of Congress do not always articulate their concerns in such bald-faced terms. Often the contestants in disputes over reorganization will take pains to camouflage or disavow any self-interest. Here again, the Carter Administration proposal to create a Department of Education offers an instructive example. The Senate Agriculture Committee—which stood to lose oversight of the child nutrition programs (such as the free lunch program) to the Senate Human Resources Committee if the programs moved to the Education Department—strongly supported efforts by the Department of Agriculture to retain control over food programs. In a letter to the Government Operations Committee, all 18 members of the Agriculture Committee warned that this and other "predatory raids" on the Agriculture Department might leave it "little more than an empty shell, incapable of serving either farmers or consumers."[9] (The reference to "predatory raids" was to other Carter Administration reorganization proposals that would strip the Agriculture Department of its food stamp program, its Soil Conservation Service, and assorted rural development programs.)[10]

Of course, not all congressional objections to executive reorganization plans are tied to the personal or subgovernmental interests of members of Congress (though these are the primary sources of opposition). Sometimes legislators will oppose a reorganization plan because they have sincere concerns about the policy consequences of a reshuffling. Some members will object if the reorganization cannot be justified in terms of greater "economy" or budget savings. Moreover, members sometimes oppose reorganization plans that strike them simply as presidential attempts to consolidate power and policy control at the expense of Congress.

In spite of these multiple sources of opposition, many reorganization proposals manage to win congressional approval. Of course, many of those are plans that would make only minor alterations in federal agencies or departments. Other plans pass because the agencies involved enjoy little or no support on Capitol Hill. Bureaus whose programs offer few tangible benefits for legislators or their constituents but still use up tax dollars will have difficulty finding widespread support in Congress. Some agencies even lack the support of committee allies. Obviously, these organizations will have trouble resisting unwelcome presidential reorganization initiatives.

Such was the case in 1971 when President Nixon proposed to consolidate federal volunteer programs—the Peace Corps and VISTA (Volunteers in Service to America)—into a new volunteer agency to be called ACTION. Volunteer groups actively lobbied to defeat the plan, arguing that an agency with such a diverse array of programs was not fundamentally sound and would thus end up serving no one well. Disagreements between VISTA and the Peace Corps were fundamental and overarching; all they could agree on was their skepticism that a consolidation of the two agencies would lead to economies, enhanced effectiveness, or other benefits.[11] But it took weeks before opponents to the reorganization could find even one senator who would lead the fight against the proposed consolidation. Their problem was clear to all; these programs had no natural constituency in Congress (indeed, the VISTA program was actually unpopular). Not surprisingly, the agencies were unable to stave off the reshuffling, and ACTION was created in July 1971.[12]

Many other agencies have had similar experiences. For example, the old U.S. Information Agency, with no natural constituency and few allies in Congress, has passed through many different (and disruptive) organizational incarnations over the years.

In sum, even though many reorganization proposals pass muster with Congress, the approval of a substantive reorganization plan is still a remarkable event because so many of them founder on the shoals of the congressional committee system; there is relatively little a president can do to enhance their safe passage.

The Reorganization Approval Process

In view of what may by now seem to be the excessive and untoward power exercised by Congress in this whole process, it is important to recall that Congress shares fully in the formal control of the bureaucracy. Although the president nominally is the head of the federal executive apparatus, the president's powers and grants of authority in organizational matters are in fact rather modest. Congress, after all, has the formal power to create agencies, reorganize them, alter their jurisdictions, or abolish them by letting their program authority lapse entirely. Thus, the congressional role in considering executive reorganization plans is part of its right and responsibility to oversee the bureaucracy. This caveat is offered not to excuse the sometimes pathologically cozy relations between congressional committees and executive agencies, but to indicate that when Congress resists plans to reorganize the bureaucracy, it is not usurping presidential authority; the authority to reorganize rests with Congress in the first place. A president can do nothing if Congress decides (as it occasionally does) to reorganize federal agencies by legislative statute.

Congress has on rare occasions chosen to delegate full reorganization powers to the president, permitting the president to implement a restructuring merely by issuing an executive order. For example, the Overman Act of 1917 accorded the president the right to reorganize in this way to facilitate the war mobilization process. However, even in this case Congress limited the president's power to reorganize, stipulating that entire bureaus could not be eliminated, existing departments could not be consolidated, and all new organizational arrangements were to be temporary, expiring six months after the war's end.[13]

Congress has also chosen on occasion to delegate authority directly to agency or department heads to permit them to carry out internal reorganizations. However, this practice is generally limited to minor adjustments or alterations in the bureaucratic machinery. Even so, the relevant congressional oversight committee may request that even these minor changes be cleared first (if only informally) with committee members.[14]

Probably the most important and conspicuous mechanism for initiating executive reorganizations is the formal submission to Congress of a presidential plan outlining a proposed reorganization. This mechanism became a fixed part of the reorganization repertoire as a result of the Reorganization Act of 1949. The Act (based on the belief, popularized by the Brownlow Commission, that responsibility for administrative management rested primarily with the president) grants the president the right to transmit reorganization plans to Congress while that body is in session. A plan would lay before both houses of Congress for a specified period, usually sixty days, after which it could be implemented unless vetoed by either the Senate or the House of Representatives. The act contained an assortment of restrictions on this presidential authority. For example, it (1) prohibited any changes or amendments to a plan once it went to Congress for consideration, (2) limited the number of plans that could be submitted to Congress in any thirty-day period and the number of matters each plan could address, and (3) prohibited the use of this authority to create new departments.

The nature of the restrictions contained in the Reorganization Act of 1949 reflects the general wariness with which members of Congress have viewed presidential reorganization initiatives. Many members of Congress remain uncomfortable with what they perceive as a reversal of the legislative process—that is, allowing a president to propose a plan, which Congress may pass on by means of a legislative veto. These concerns are exacerbated by the nature of this veto mechanism, which confers a greater advantage on the White House than on possible opponents in Congress. Under the provisions of the law, a presidential proposal takes effect automatically unless either house of Congress *disapproves* it. Since the legislative process is unusually slow and ponderous in our political system, with the greatest political burden on those who must put together a majority coalition, the advantage in this case lies with the president. If the veto mechanism were of another form—if, for example, a reorganization plan would take effect only if one (or both) houses of Congress *approved* the plan—the advantage would rest with congressional opponents since the burden would then be on the White House to assemble a coalition in support of its plan. As it is now, however, the *procedural* advantage rests with the president.

It is little wonder, then, that many members of Congress greet with suspicion presidential requests for grants of further reorganization authority or for an easing of restrictions on their authority. For example, in 1977 President Carter asked Congress to renew his authority under the Reorganization Act of 1949. (Congress had permitted it to lapse in 1973 because of members' reluctance to accord President Nixon any unnecessary powers over the executive branch.) Carter also asked that the presidential reorganization authority be liberalized. He proposed a four-year renewal instead of the usual two-year extension. He wanted the right to submit plans that dealt with more than one organizational matter, he wanted a removal of the limitation on the number of plans that could be sent to Capitol Hill in any given time period, and, finally, he wanted the right to amend or change a plan once it had been submitted, in response to concerns or objections raised.[15] In the process, however, Carter learned, as presidents have before him, that it is difficult to extract further concessions from Congress on these matters.

Congress did grant Carter some of what he wanted: the new extension was for three years, and plans would be amendable within the first thirty days of their submission. At the same time, however, Congress strengthened its own hand in the whole process. Although Congress did not go so far as to institute the affirmative veto (the alternative mechanism outlined above), the legislators did require that there be an automatic introduction of a disapproval resolution in each house to ensure a floor vote on every reorganization plan.[16] This provision ensures that members who may favor a reorganization plan cannot delay a committee vote until the required sixty days have safely passed.

Overcoming Congressional Opposition

Presidents bent on reorganization face formidable obstacles on Capitol Hill and have few means at their disposal (other than some procedural advantages) for shepherding a proposal through Congress unscathed. As on all matters, of course, presidents must rely heavily on their own "powers to persuade"—to cajole and argue, but mostly to bargain.[17] Richard Neustadt has stated the case better than anyone:[18]

> *The essence of a President's persuasive task with congressmen, and everybody else,* is to induce them to believe that what he wants of them is what their own appraisal of their own responsibilities requires them to do in their interest, not his. *Because men may differ in their views on public policy, because differences in outlook stem from differences in duty—duty to one's office, one's constituents, oneself—that task is bound to be more like collective bargaining than like a reasoned argument among philosopher kings.* . . . *Persuasion deals in the coin of self-interest with men who have some freedom to reject what they find counterfeit.*

Thus, perhaps the most effective step a president can take to enhance the chances of legislative approval for a reorganization proposal is to minimize its threat to established congressional interests. This point seems to be intuitively obvious, yet it is one that is apparently lost on presidents (and their advisers) who initiate grand reorganizations as if they believe the sheer logical force of their arguments will be sufficient to carry the day. As Neustadt's comments suggest, reasoned argument will enjoy little currency when self-interest is the coin of the realm.

Presidents who want to see their reorganization initiatives win congressional approval should thus be guided by the following decision rules:

1. *Avoid sweeping reorganization proposals that aim to achieve large-scale changes in the structure of the executive branch.* The self-protective instincts of the agencies and individual congressional committees are formidable enough without incurring the hostile opposition of the whole Congress. Yet presidents seem not to learn from the experiences of their predecessors in this regard. President Nixon attracted massive opposition from Congress (and many other quarters) by his 1971 proposal to reorganize most of

the executive branch, retaining the departments of State, Treasury, Defense, and Justice, but reshuffling all of the other departments into four new super-departments of Natural Resources, Human Resources, Economic Affairs, and Community Development. However logical and well-reasoned the plan may have been, it was a blueprint for political disaster. The panoply of interest groups and executive agencies fueled congressional opposition; even the enthusiastic sponsorship of Senator Abraham Ribicoff (D.–Conn.) and Representative Chet Holifield (D.–Calif.), chairmen of the government operations units in each chamber, was insufficient to stem the swollen tide of congressional opposition.

Sometimes, of course, a president manages to win congressional acceptance of a large-scale reorganization plan in spite of strong resistance from various quarters on Capitol Hill. But such success occurs rarely and only in the presence of exceptional circumstances, such as a crisis atmosphere (which facilitated congressional approval of a new Department of Energy in 1977) or the support of an exceptionally powerful clientele group. For example, the Carter Administration's proposal to consolidate the many disparate programs and agencies having to do with education into a new Department of Education managed to overcome initial congressional opposition because of the extraordinary power of the National Education Association, the national teachers' organization that vigorously supported the plan. In this case, members of Congress recognized that their political self-interest rested more with protecting their reelection chances than with worrying about disruptions to their committee jurisdictions.

2. *Follow the rules of the game; violating established procedures only adds insult to injury.* In 1979 (in a move reminiscent of Nixon's eight years earlier), President Carter called for a vast new Department of Natural Resources that would have absorbed the entire Department of Interior and large elements of the Agriculture and Commerce Departments, thus giving the new organization more comprehensive authority over the whole range of America's land resources, national parks and forests, continental shelf, and oceanic areas. Carter's plan encountered the inevitable opposition from members of the Agriculture and Commerce committees in both houses of Congress.

But Carter and his advisers also aroused the strident opposition of the Senate Governmental Affairs Committee by choosing to submit a plan to Congress under the terms of the president's re-organization plan authority, rather than to ask Congress for legis-lation enacting the change. Normally, establishing a new depart-ment requires congressional passage of new legislation. But the Carter Administration claimed that its plan was simply a renaming and reorganizing of an existing department and thus fell within the range of the president's delegated authority to propose a plan that would take effect unless vetoed by either house of Congress. Senator Ribicoff, still chairman of the Senate Governmental Af-fairs Committee, warned:[19]

> *I think it's a sure way of getting the back of Congress up by doing it that way. . . . Whatever has to be done to reject it will be done. My committee feels very strongly that changing any programs from one department to another or basically changing the mission of a department should be done by law. If you want to make changes like this, you should go the statutory route.*

3. *Be willing to bargain, compromise, or back down in order to achieve some goals.* Members of Congress are not innately ob-structive. As politicians, they recognize that the exercise of power involves bargaining and compromise. Thus, presidents may en-hance their chances of winning what they want in the way of executive reorganizations if they are willing to refrain from making too many demands on Congress at once and if they are willing to drop provisions that pose special problems for legislators.

For example, just before they proposed creation of a Depart-ment of Natural Resources, President Carter and his reorganiza-tion advisers decided to reject another major reorganization pro-posal that (again, like the earlier Nixon plan) would have established a new Department of Development Assistance to consolidate most of the community development programs and urban-oriented economic programs under one agency. Early po-litical soundings convinced the White House that the plan could never survive on Capitol Hill, so the president jettisoned the idea, in part to avoid damaging the prospects for his other proposals (such as the plan to create the Department of Education), which were already encountering resistance on the Hill.

Even more to the point is the case of Nixon's plan to create the new volunteer agency, ACTION. One reason the Nixon Admin-istration successfully skirted congressional opposition to the plan is that the president and his advisers agreed to exclude from it the

Teachers Corps, a program then located in the Office of Education in the Department of Health, Education, and Welfare. Key committee members from both houses of Congress had made it clear to the Administration that should the teacher-training program be included in the new volunteer agency, they would have no choice but to fight for rejection of the entire plan. The Nixon Administration officials excluded the Teachers Corps, thus salvaging the major parts of the plan.

Summary

Congress has long recognized a president's need, on occasion, to reorganize the executive branch in the name of better management. But Congress also recognizes that control of the federal bureaucracy is a shared function, and it repeatedly reminds presidents of that by keeping tight rein on the nature and scope of presidential reorganization proposals. The history of presidential-congressional battles over executive organization is rich (though barely tapped by scholars). Its lesson for presidents intent on reorganization is clear: the key to winning congressional approval lies foremost in convincing legislators that their own personal power stakes and their supportive relationships with allies in the bureaucracy will not be imperiled by a proposed change. This is no small feat; it requires political sensitivity of the first order, including the ability to cajole, persuade, bargain, and compromise. And, not least, it requires presidential acknowledgment that control over the executive branch is not a president's exclusive preserve.

Endnotes

1. Harold Seidman, *Politics, Position, and Power*, 3d ed. (New York: Oxford University Press, 1980), p. 40.
2. *Ibid.*, p. 70.
3. Douglass Cater, *Power in Washington* (New York: Random House, 1964).
4. James Q. Wilson, *The Investigators* (New York: Basic Books, 1978), p. 164.

5. Lawrence C. Dodd and Richard L. Schott, *Congress and the Administrative State* (New York: John Wiley & Sons, 1979), p. 326.
6. Joseph A. Califano, Jr., *A Presidential Nation* (New York: W. W. Norton & Co., 1975), pp. 24–25.
7. As quoted in Seidman, *Politics, Position, and Power*, p. 48.
8. *Ibid.*, pp. 48–49.
9. Joel Havemann, "Carter's Reorganization Plans—Scrambling for Turf," *The National Journal*, May 20, 1978, p. 791.
10. *Ibid.*
11. Jamie Heard, "Plan to Merge VISTA, Peace Corps, Other Volunteer Programs Nears Approval," *The National Journal*, May 15, 1971, pp. 1048–51.
12. While opponents of the reorganization were unable to win enough congressional support to defeat the plan, they were able to convince Congress to extract one concession from the administration—the separate identities of the programs to be merged would be preserved. See Michael P. Balzano, *Reorganizing the Federal Bureaucracy, The Rhetoric and the Reality* (Washington, D.C.: American Enterprise Institute for Public Policy Research, 1977).
13. Dodd and Schott, *Congress and the Administrative State*, pp. 331–32.
14. *Ibid.*, p. 333.
15. Herbert Kaufman, "Reflections on Administrative Reorganization," in Frederick S. Lane, ed., *Current Issues in Public Administration* (New York: St. Martin's Press, 1978), pp. 217–18.
16. Dodd and Schott, *Congress and the Administrative State*, p. 335.
17. Richard E. Neustadt, *Presidential Power* (New York: John Wiley & Sons, 1980), pp. 26–29.
18. *Ibid.*, p. 35.
19. Quoted in *The New York Times*, March 1, 1979, p. D 16.

Chapter 4

REORGANIZATION: THE AGENCY'S PERSPECTIVE

The targets of executive reorganizations, federal agencies, can often be painful thorns in the side of a president seeking to reorganize. In fact, the fear of bureaucratic opposition scuttling a plan may lead the White House to take defensive actions that in turn may create much hostility and suspicion on the part of those bureaucrats to be affected. Staff members charged with developing a reorganization may be wary of tipping their hand in advance of a formal unveiling of a plan, lest opponents be given an opportunity to unite and mobilize support for their position. However, the failure to invite agency involvement in the early stages of a plan's development can lead to another set of problems. Agencies and their friends and supporters may charge the reorganization's early architects with secrecy and misrepresentation—charges that may provoke sympathetic reactions on Capitol Hill and the possibility of congressional rejection of a plan.

The dilemma faced by reorganizers is not one easily solved. Hostile agency attitudes toward reorganization are well documented, and examples of successful agency efforts to impede proposed plans are plentiful. Concern by bureaucrats over their own job status and civil service rank is perhaps the most commonly articulated explanation for agency opposition to reorganization. But the reasons for bureaucratic apprehension over the prospect of a reorganization are usually more diverse. They include the desire to protect organizational autonomy, anxieties about the protection of an agency's ethos or sense of mission, and concerns about the possible rupturing of mutually beneficial relationships between an agency, its protective clientele or interest groups, and relevant congressional committees and subcommittees.

Protecting Agency Autonomy

In recent decades, federal executive agencies have become powerful political entities. Public bureaucracies, acting with the legitimate authority of the state, regulate a wide range of behavior and products in American society and make choices that lead to the conferral of costs and benefits on certain individuals and groups. In the course of making or implementing those decisions, agencies often exercise wide discretion. This discretion, and the expertise used in exercising it, makes federal agencies powerful institutions.

Accompanying the increased power of the federal bureaucratic establishment are heightened criticisms of agency behavior. Politicians and the public alike criticize the bureaucracy for being impersonal, parochial, self-protective, and strangled in its own "red tape." Adding to this largely negative view of bureaucracy are notions that government agencies are "imperialistic"—unwaveringly seeking expanded powers and jurisdictions, larger budgets, more staff, or increases in other organizational resources.[1] In fact, this notion of bureaucratic imperialism has now come to dominate both the scholarly and the popular views about how public agencies behave.

Yet an alternative view—and one that adds to our understanding of why agencies tend to resist reorganization—suggests that although an agency will naturally prefer more rather than less authority or resources, the primary goal of a federal bureau is to seek a maximum of organizational *autonomy*. An agency enjoys autonomy when it (1) enjoys sole jurisdiction over a certain set of tasks or (2) can "act independently of some or all of the groups that have the authority to constrain it."[2] Both kinds of bureaucratic autonomy can be difficult to achieve in a governmental system characterized by fragmentation of power and authority. Both kinds can be threatened as well by a reorganization that proposes alterations in an agency's departmental location, structure, or tasks.

Sole jurisdiction over a coherent set of tasks is elusive because the federal executive branch is studded with agencies that have overlapping jurisdictions and similar tasks. The administrative history of the federal government is replete with stories of agencies locking horns over organizational "turf." Perhaps the classic case is the celebrated struggle between the Army Corps of Engineers and the Interior Department's Bureau of Reclamation for jurisdiction over water resource projects and development of the nation's waterways.[3] More recently, the Department of Health and Human Services (formerly Health, Education, and Welfare) has struggled with the Department of Agriculture for control of nutrition and food inspection programs, each department claiming that it should be given control of programs now in the other. The rivalry between the Bureau of Narcotics and Dangerous Drugs and the U.S. Customs Service for the lead role in federal narcotics enforcement activities—the subject of a detailed analysis in later chapters—led to such intense squabbling and battles for the superior organizational position that a reorganization was finally settled on in hopes of solving the bitter turf battle.

All of these examples are not so much ones of bureaucratic imperialism as instances of agencies seeking to secure a legally and politically recognized area of distinctive competence in which other organizations do not intrude. Autonomy is obviously preferable to competition or confused jurisdiction because an agency that enjoys the former will have a stronger claim on the support of outside interest groups and a better chance at winning congressional and presidential favor. Reorganizations aimed at resolving such disputes by designating one agency as the sole inheritor of a set of jurisdictions will be well received by the organization whose autonomy is to be enhanced. But such plans will be forcefully resisted by the other organization faced with the prospect of curtailed authority or the weakening of its autonomy.

The search for bureaucratic autonomy also helps to explain other instances of agency behavior that cannot be adequately accounted for by the "bureaucratic imperialism" view of public bureaucracies. For example, the Federal Bureau of Investigation refused throughout J. Edgar Hoover's rule (and for a time thereafter) to become involved in investigating either organized crime or narcotics trafficking. Such expansions of the FBI's investigative activities would have required it to engage in "collaborative ventures with other agencies that were or might become rivals." As James Q. Wilson explains: "Hoover knew instinctively what every natural executive knows: having a monopoly on even a small piece of turf is better than having a competitive position on a larger one."[4]

Agencies' preferences for autonomy (even over resources) also help explain an otherwise puzzling anomaly presented by Morton Halperin: The chiefs of the military services in the 1960s were unhappy with Secretary of Defense Robert McNamara even though he substantially *increased* their budgets; yet they approved of his successor, Melvin Laird, even though Laird *cut* their budgets. Pentagon morale was better under Laird because he increased the autonomy of the services; it was worse under McNamara because he reduced the services' autonomy.[5]

What these examples show is that government agencies value organizational autonomy because for them it is such a scarce resource. As a result, much of the political activity in Washington (especially that which is most confusing to outside observers) consists of agencies struggling, with the support of allies in and outside of government, to enhance or maintain their autonomy. Agencies pursue avenues to broaden their power base, including, on occasion, the instigation of calls for reorganizations (as has happened with the U.S. Customs Service), not because their members are megalomaniacs but because the tremendous fragmentation of power and authority in the American system of government makes it difficult for an agency to conduct its activities with consistency, efficiency, and coherence. To reduce the unpredictability of their environments and to pursue their given goals more effectively, agencies seek autonomy—at the least, an assured jurisdiction over a coherent set of tasks. Better yet, they seek a measure of independence and protection from the constraints imposed by other political institutions. An agency's quest for autonomy, or its defensive posture against actions that would threaten what autonomy it does possess, offers one cogent explanation for the distaste so often evidenced by bureaucracies over reorganizations.

Protecting Subsystem Relationships

Another reason why agencies are so predictably loath to embrace reorganization centers on their desire to protect their existing relationships with supportive interests outside the government and in Congress. Indeed, the degree of autonomy enjoyed by a governmental unit may well be affected by the strength of its external support network. The kind and extent of support generated by the public at large, specific interest or clientele groups, and friends on relevant congressional committees can have an important bearing on the chances of a bureaucracy successfully defending itself against a proposed reorganization, especially one disruptive to a carefully nurtured set of mutually beneficial relationships with outside interests. For example, Francis E. Rourke argues that an agency that enjoys general public support should be in a better position to extract autonomy and resources from other political elites or institutions. He notes:[6]

> *Since public opinion is ultimately the only legitimate sovereign in a democratic society, an agency that seeks first a high standing with the public can reasonably expect to have things handed to it in the way of legislative and executive support. Power gives power, in administration as elsewhere, and once an agency has established a secure base with the public, it cannot be easily trifled with by political officials in either the legislative or executive branch.*

Public opinion is remarkably fickle, however, and an agency concerned about maintaining its position and status by averting reorganizations that threaten autonomy or established relations with an outside support system will seek more special assistance from those groups that are directly affected by the programs the agency administers. For example, the Department of Agriculture naturally has the support of many farmers; the Defense Department cultivates mutually beneficial relationships with defense-related industries; the Office for Civil Rights draws support and encouragement from women's groups.

Depending on the nature of an agency's task and political environment, its clientele may consist not of a single, powerful ally, but of a number of competing groups. A multigroup clientele may allow an agency greater discretion in staking out policy positions since it may play one interest's demands against another's, confident that whatever action it takes, at least some of its clients will support it. But since an agency needs strong clientele support to extract concessions from, or to ward off, other political elites, an agency will naturally prefer a large actively supportive clientele (therefore possessing more potential electoral influence) that is widely dispersed geographically (preferably spread over most or all congressional districts) and professionally respectable (and thus in a better position to command the attention of political elites).

Of course, not all agencies have cozy relationships with congressional committees and interest groups. Some organizations, such as VISTA, have found it difficult to generate much support on Capitol Hill. Other organizations have outright hostile relationships with interest groups. The powerful gun lobby's attacks on the Bureau of Alcohol, Tobacco, and Firearms in the Treasury Department is one example; the constant battles between environmentalist groups and the James Watt–led Interior Department is another.

By successfully cultivating support from the general and specific publics and from Congress, an agency improves its chances of securing greater autonomy within the executive branch. That support and the enhanced autonomy it brings can then become a valuable asset in avoiding attempts by the White House to reorganize these well-connected agencies. For example, the FBI's successful attempts (until 1981 when its attitude and public posture changed) to thwart those interested in attaching narcotics law enforcement to its list of responsibilities were aided by the "almost unparalleled degree of autonomy" enjoyed by the agency until the mid-1970s. As one close observer of the FBI has explained: "Part of the reason it achieved such substantial freedom from criticism is that it anticipated the needs and cultivated the support of key elected officials, chiefly congressmen."[7]

In short, to secure autonomy and resources necessary to withstand perceived threats to its standing in the political system, an agency will seek to nurture favor and goodwill from the general public and from its specific clientele groups, and will cultivate supportive alliances in Congress.

Interest Group Response to Threats of Reorganization

All of this helps to explain why it is so common for outside interests to rally around an agency designated as a candidate for reorganization. Although agencies have much to lose by the threat of a reorganization disruptive to subsystem relationships, so, too, do groups whose interests are protected or promoted by a particular agency or department. The fact that a reorganization may cause favored programs to lose visibility or prestige, or the fear that a restructuring may result in lower appropriations or signify a change in policy emphasis, can be all the impetus needed for a clientele group to mobilize an intense effort to undercut attempts at executive reorganization.

When Jimmy Carter first proposed creation of a cabinet-level Department of Education in 1978, a wide array of groups of differing power and status promptly emerged to lead the battle to prevent agencies (with which they had special ties) from being swallowed by the new unit. Supporters of the Head Start program were just one group immediately public and vocal in opposition to the proposed reorganization. The Children's Defense Fund, Inc., a public interest charity working to protect the interests of children, argued that to relocate Head Start might well have negative effects on the nontraditional educational program, leading to its transformation into just another "narrow classroom program" lost in the "rigidities" of a formal education establishment.[8] The politically more powerful and well-financed veterans' lobby pressured for the exclusion of the Veterans Administration's educational programs from the Education Department as well. This group feared the potential loss of "one-stop shopping" at the VA and the potential deemphasis of educational programs for veterans in general if such programs were to be consolidated into a large department with interests ranging far afield of the needs of veterans.[9]

The desire of vested interests to protect agencies and their programs important to their membership also helps to account for the largely negative reaction to President Richard Nixon's attempt in 1971 to create a new Department of Community Development. Powerful lobbies, ranging from farm groups to highway interests, mobilized their constituencies to pressure the government to reject plans that would lead to a relocation of agencies administering programs and policies of special interest to them. Again, the foremost fear was that "their" programs would lose prestige, resources, and attention if consolidated into a huge bureaucracy with far-flung and diverse responsibilities. Naturally, agencies find the threat of subordination to a much larger governmental unit as disagreeable as the interest groups whom they court. In the case of the proposed Department of Community Development, the Nixon Administration learned just how powerful such opposition could be. Highway interests argued that the new bureaucracy would not place nearly as much emphasis on highways as had the Transportation Department; farmers' lobbies were able to raise the ire of their supporters and were able to feed opposition to the reorganization by questioning the future of rural development programs if transferred to the new department (even going so far as to suggest that one purpose of the proposed reorganization might have been the future elimination of the entire Department of Agriculture).[10] The eventual scuttling of plans to create the new cabinet department was no doubt due, at least in part, to the forceful opposition mounted by these groups and the sympathetic response such concerns were able to raise among members of Congress—especially among the chairpersons of those committees with jurisdiction over the agencies and programs slated to be transferred.[11]

The opposition an administration bent on reorganization encounters does not end with organized groups in the private sector. State governments, city mayors, and various bureaucratic units below the federal level may all be "clients" or beneficiaries of various federal programs and agencies as well—and thus anxious to guard against changes that would affect the structural pipeline sending federal aid to their level of government. For example, when the Carter Administration drew up a comprehensive plan to consolidate twelve programs scattered in three different cabinet departments dealing with economic and community development, the heat of opposition was immediately felt from urban areas. Carter staff members were proposing that the Department of Housing and Urban Development be expanded into a "Department of Development Assistance." The existing structure of HUD would be maintained, but that department would also acquire a myriad of additional agencies and programs —including the Economic Development Administration, parts of the Farmers Home Administration, and various other economic development activities from such organizations as the Small Business Administration and the Community Services Administration.

The response from state and urban officials was not favorable. HUD itself had never enjoyed a high rating from urban officials; they viewed it as the prime example of an inefficient, cumbersome, and slow bureaucracy. Nevertheless, the idea of augmenting this department's responsibilities disturbed many urban officials who liked having an organization geared solely toward their own urban interests, and they lobbied hard against the proposed restructuring. Buttressed by the support of the rural lobby, these officials argued that both urban and rural goals might well be diluted by folding them into one massive organization with many other functions also competing for attention.[12]

Another example of the strong response federal reorganization can elicit from public sector interests was the Carter Administration's proposal to consolidate five major disaster agencies into one, the Federal Emergency Management Agency. Some groups were enthusiastic in their support for the new organization, including the American Red Cross and the National Governors' Association. But strong opposition arose from various city mayors and urban lobbying groups to the proposed plan to merge fire prevention, disaster relief, and civil defense programs into the one new lead agency. The National League of Cities, for example, opposed the transferal of the National Fire Prevention and Control Administration (NFPCA), arguing that such a proposal indicated a misunderstanding of NFPCA and the problems and needs of cities attempting to respond to the demands of fire protection.[13] The League was also vehement in its belief that to remove NFPCA from its home in the Commerce Department only further underscored the failure of the Administration to recognize the importance of leaving undisturbed an agency whose institutional environment was supportive of its goals and orientation.

These examples serve to emphasize the depth and breadth of the opposition outside interests can muster in an effort to dissuade an administration—or Congress—of the desirability of an impending reorganization plan. These organized groups often seem

to have a highly developed sixth sense for catching wind of reorganizations that threaten projects or programs in which they
hold a particular interest. The lobbying can be fierce and the
winning of sympathetic members of Congress relatively easy,
especially if a proposed reorganization would either affect congressional committee jurisdictions or the pet agencies or projects
of certain powerful representatives in the legislative branch. For
a president and his staff one obvious response would seem to be
an aggressive lobbying effort of their own. But while such a tactic
may appeal to administration officials dismayed by the efforts of
special interests to undermine a serious reorganization attempt, a
president must weigh carefully the costs and benefits of waging
an expensive battle with these groups. In fact, the mere threat or
warning of a challenge to an executive reorganization plan by a
well-established and influential lobby may be all that is necessary
to delete or exempt certain agencies from a plan in which they
logically seem to belong.

Instances in which a reorganization, even in its preliminary
stages, has been scuttled by vocal public opposition—and the
hesitancy of an administration to take on these opponents—are
not infrequent. For example, the Carter Administration was forced
to drop plans to reorganize border patrol authorities in 1978 because of pressures brought by the National Border Patrol Council.
The council, representing personnel of the Immigration and Naturalization Service, was able to convince its friends in Congress,
most notably the members of the House Judiciary Committee,
that such a move would result in "chaos" if the jurisdiction of
INS were carved up and shared with the U.S. Customs Service.
If the reorganization were carried out, the Judiciary Committee
would have lost its oversight responsibility over INS to the House
Ways and Means Committee. This likelihood no doubt con-
tributed to the committee's decision to inform the White House
of its opposition to the move.[14] The Carter Administration, un-
willing to engage in battle with Peter Rodino (D.–N.J.), chairman of the Judiciary Committee, concluded that the best strategy
was to retire the plan for "further study." And even if a special
interest fails to snatch a favorite governmental unit from under
the reorganization scalpel, the agency may still win concessions
or compromises from the administration on the location or nature
of the incisions.

In sum, the political subsystems of our government (referred to by some as "iron triangles" or "triple alliances"), which wed agencies, special interests, and congressional committees around a particular cause or program, may present a most formidable obstacle to a president intent on executive branch reorganization. Presidential attempts to revamp organizational structures will always risk raising the ire of at least one of the components of these subsystems, if not all three. Agencies concerned about both the maintenance of their autonomy and the continued existence of key ties with supportive groups in and outside government present one potentially critical hurdle; special interest or clientele groups anxious to protect carefully nurtured and mutually beneficial relationships with agencies and friends on Capitol Hill offer a second source of opposition; and, as the previous chapter indicates, congressional committees, protective of their own "turf" or suspicious of policy changes camouflaged by reorganization rhetoric, constitute yet a third possible source of opposition to executive reorganization.

Protecting Mission and Agency Ethos

Yet another explanation for agency resistance to reorganization stems from the reluctance of agency personnel to alter deep-rooted methods of operation. Organizations that have a firmly established sense of their "mission" or "distinctive competence" are considered to be among the easiest organizations to manage.[15] But these can also be among the most difficult to change. In such agencies there is generally "a widely shared view among organization members as to the nature, feasibility, and importance of the organization's principal tasks."[16] As a result, morale tends to be high, and managers need to expend less time inducing the required commitments of organization members. To management, then, a highly developed sense of mission is a most welcome asset.

But a strong sense of mission or a deeply institutionalized agency ethos also carries drawback. It can make the acceptance of change most difficult for operators within an agency slated for reorganization. This would be especially true for those agencies whose operational norms and keen sense of mission are used in the socialization process of agency personnel. To effect a change that would disrupt such a process or shatter an agency's view of accepted behavior, norms, and incentives may well carry costs far in excess of any gains the reorganization could achieve. So, a reorganization plan perceived as a threat to an organization's mission is sure to be resisted vigorously—and not only because agency personnel may be "afraid of change" or are simply desirous of maintaining a certain civil service rank. Rather, opposition to the reorganization may stem from the perceived need to protect a secure sense of identity and the set of values and agreements that help give form to that identity.

Examples of agencies determined to rebuff reorganization plans that threaten their organizational mission or ethos are not hard to find. For instance, the FBI's refusal to add narcotics functions to its existing set of tasks was no doubt based not only on a desire by Hoover to protect and maintain the agency's autonomy, but also on a desire to preserve the strong sense of mission held by his agents. The FBI's behavior, identity, and attitude toward its tasks were of a markedly different nature than that of the lead narcotics agency. Hoover, and others who succeeded him, feared substantial internal disruptions, if not the "corruption" of the agency, if forced to accept into the FBI agents adhering to a different and far less strict code of conduct.[17]

The Forest Service is another organization that is known to have a strong, well-established sense of mission and organizational identity. This agency, too, has repeatedly opposed reorganization proposals that it views as a threat to its standards and organizational ethos. It did so, for example, in 1971 when the Nixon Administration wanted to remove the Forest Service from the Department of Agriculture and place it in a new Department of Natural Resources. The leaders of the agency lost no time in making clear how distasteful such a move would be, especially if forced to merge with the Interior Department. The Forest Service had opposed for many years efforts to move it into Interior because of Interior's orientation, which the Forest Service believed not to be consistent with its own attitudes and beliefs.[18]

In sum, the emergence of a highly developed sense of mission or firmly established agency ethos can be a double-edged sword: It may well ease the managerial task because of the consensus it promotes within the organization, but at the cost of cultivating a strong bed of resistance to change.

Summary

Every president who seeks to reorganize the executive branch must be prepared to respond to hostile reactions and the negative attitudes of bureaucrats whose organizations are to be affected. A president or his staff may try to disarm or placate an organization upset at the prospect of reorganization. The administration's attempts may take a variety of forms: (1) assigning career-level bureaucrats to the reorganization team, (2) inviting formal agency responses to preliminary reorganization blueprints, or (3) promising to make reorganization "painless"—as Jimmy Carter did in 1977 when he vowed that his streamlining of the executive branch would result in no firings or demotions of federal employees.[19]

Whether such strategies can be repeatedly successful in diluting or erasing agency opposition to proposed reorganizations is of some doubt. Certainly there are times when a reorganization may be warmly embraced by an organization—if, for example, it enhances the visibility or status of programs administered by that unit or if it will confer greater autonomy on the agency. But, as this chapter shows, bureaucratic resistance to reorganization is the more common reaction. And it has roots that run much deeper than to such facile explanations of agency hostility as "simple fear of change" or fear of loss of a civil service rank. Concern for the protection of bureaucratic autonomy, a shared desire among federal agencies, supportive outside interests, and congressional committees to maintain the carefully built and nurtured political subsystems of our government, and the fear of a weakened sense of mission or agency ethos are all additional—and more important factors—that help explain bureaucratic distaste for reorganization. The nature of these obstacles makes the president's task of reorganization more difficult in terms of winning approval of various plans, hinders implementation of such plans, and produces consequences of reorganization both unintended and unanticipated.

The next chapter begins an in-depth analysis of one major and serious attempt at presidential reorganization. This discussion should more clearly illuminate the perspective of the federal bureaucracy toward reorganization, the tactics agencies can employ in attempts to thwart presidential restructuring, and the kinds of unintended consequences reorganization can cause.

Endnotes

1. See, for example, Matthew Holden, Jr., " 'Imperialism' in Bureaucracy," in Francis E. Rourke, ed., *Bureaucratic Power in National Politics*, 3d ed. (Boston: Little, Brown, & Co., 1978), pp. 164–81.
2. James Q. Wilson, *The Investigators* (New York: Basic Books, 1978), p. 165.
3. Arthur Maass, *Muddy Waters* (Cambridge, Mass.: Harvard University Press, 1951).
4. Wilson, *The Investigators*, p. 170.
5. Morton H. Halperin, *Bureaucratic Politics and Foreign Policy* (Washington, D.C.: The Brookings Institution, 1974), pp. 51–54.
6. Francis E. Rourke, *Bureaucracy, Politics, and Public Policy*, 2d ed. (Boston: Little, Brown, & Co., 1976), pp. 43–44.
7. Wilson, *The Investigators*, p. 166. There are, of course, some agencies that command no strong support from Congress or the public and are thus reliant almost exclusively on presidential support and confidence if they are to achieve any independent standing. See Francis Rourke, *Bureaucracy, Politics, and Public Policy*, p. 65.
8. Joel Havemann, "Carter Reorganization Plans—Scrambling for Turf," *The National Journal*, May 20, 1978, p. 790.
9. *Ibid.*, p. 792.
10. William Lilley, III, "Hostile Committee Chairmen, Lobbies Pledge Fight Against Reorganization Plan," *The National Journal*, October 16, 1971, pp. 2074–75.
11. *Ibid.*, p. 2080.
12. Rochelle L. Stanfield, "The Best Laid Reorganization Plans Sometimes Go Astray," *The National Journal*, January 20, 1979, p. 89.
13. S. Scott Rohrer, "The Disaster Reorganization Plan Takes on an Organizational Disaster," *The National Journal*, July 8, 1978, pp. 1088–89.
14. Joel Havemann, "Carter's Reorganization Plans—Scrambling for Turf," p. 794.
15. See, for example, Wilson, *The Investigators*, pp. 13–14; Herbert Kaufman, *The Forest Ranger* (Baltimore: The Johns Hopkins University Press, 1960), pp. 476–78; Lester Salamon, "The Goals of Reorganization, A Framework for Analysis," *Administration and Society* 12 (February 1981); and Philip Selznick, *Leadership in Administration* (New York: Harper & Row, 1957), pp. 42–56.
16. Wilson, *The Investigators*, p. 13.
17. *Ibid.*, p. 212.
18. Dom Bonafede, "Bureaucracy, Congress, Interests See Threat in Nixon Reorganization Plan," *The National Journal*, May 8, 1971, p. 980.
19. Joel Havemann, "Can Carter Chop Through the Civil Service System?" *The National Journal*, April 23, 1977, p. 618.

Chapter 5

A CASE IN POINT: THE 1973 REORGANIZATION OF FEDERAL NARCOTICS ENFORCEMENT AGENCIES

Reorganization Plan No. 2 of 1973 was a serious, well-intentioned effort to change the way federal narcotics law enforcement agencies were performing their functions. It was not simply an attempt to change personnel or to achieve cosmetic changes in the narcotics arena, nor was its primary purpose merely to present the appearance of change for political reasons. Rather, the 1973 reorganization plan was specifically designed to consolidate (and thereby alter the nature of) federal narcotics enforcement activities into one lead agency, the Drug Enforcement Administration (DEA). The expectation was that a new alignment of agencies and jurisdictions would improve significantly the efficiency and effectiveness of the federal government's drug enforcement program.

Political stakes were also involved, however, because the narcotics law enforcement effort was linked directly to President Richard Nixon's "war on heroin," to which the president had attached high priority. Accordingly, this reorganization presents an interesting and informative case study. It illustrates the difficulty of engineering reorganizations that can achieve the desired results, and it also shows the pitfalls and obstacles that lie in the path of most reorganization plans.

The Call for Reorganization

The Nixon Administration transmitted Reorganization Plan No. 2 to Congress on March 28, 1973. The message accompanying the plan's unveiling underscored the president's determination to wage the "war against drugs" with great vigor. In calling for congressional approval of the proposed reorganization, President Nixon used the opportunity to renew his pledge to preserve the top-priority status of his Administration's "all-out, global war on the drug menace," and the proposed organizational changes were to serve as proof of his desire to intensify the fight against drugs.[1]

More importantly, the proponents of the plan expected the reorganization of agency jurisdictions to end what they considered to be a counterproductive rivalry between the agents of the Bureau of Narcotics and Dangerous Drugs (BNDD) in the Justice Department and the U.S. Customs Service in the Treasury Department. The reorganization's architects believed that decentralized authority and jurisdictional overlap—both the result of the multiplicity of agencies involved in antidrug efforts—encouraged bureaucratic competition that was severely hampering drug enforcement activities. Administration officials' interpretation of the available evidence led them to believe that the two principal organizations involved, BNDD and Customs, were behaving in a manner that could be deemed detrimental to "good government." The Office of Management and Budget (OMB) and the General Accounting Office (GAO) identified a number of problems plaguing these two agencies: (1) alleged sabotaging by one agency of a rival's case; (2) lack of communication, coordination, and cooperation between BNDD and Customs; and (3) overlap in missions involving at least nine federal agencies. The Administration contended that the reorganization was the cathartic needed to correct these problems permanently.

Thus, Reorganization Plan No. 2 of 1973 was conceived as an effort to achieve these two goals: consolidation of narcotics authority and elimination of duplicative and overlapping missions. The plan proposed a realignment of legal authority among the agencies involved in narcotics law enforcement to establish a new, lead narcotics unit in the Justice Department. BNDD was to provide the personnel and organizational foundation for the new agency. In addition, a transfer of personnel—a movement of special agents from Customs to DEA and of inspectors from the Immigration and Naturalization Service (INS) to Customs— would complete the strengthening and streamlining of federal drug law enforcement activities.

The plan was in no sense presented as an economy measure, although a reduction in administrative overhead (as a result of the consolidation of certain field offices) was likely. Rather, the reorganization was justified by reference to the traditional Hoover Commission reorganization rationale—that is, to the idea that two fundamental objectives of management, efficiency and effectiveness, were being undermined by the existing structure of the federal attack on narcotics. The plan was drafted with an eye toward eliminating wasteful bureaucratic competition, minimizing any overlaps in jurisdiction (since that invites duplication of tasks), and combining like functions and purposes in one lead agency (to improve accountability and control).

What follows is, first, a further examination of the theoretical underpinnings of the reorganization proposal and, second, an analysis of the political considerations that had an important effect on the timing and structure of the reorganization proposal.

Organizational Reasons for Change

Autonomy Disputes

Proponents of reorganization singled out the bureaucratic rivalry and competition issue as the most compelling argument for change. Interdepartmental quarreling was not a new phenomenon in federal narcotics activities. As early as the mid-1930s, the Federal Bureau of Narcotics (FBN), BNDD's predecessor, and the Bureau of Customs earned reputations as jealous and combative siblings because of their jockeying within the Treasury Department for authority to control the importation and distribution of illicit drugs. An executive reorganization in 1968 transferred the tasks and personnel of FBN out of Treasury and into the newly created BNDD in the Justice Department. As exasperated OMB officials quickly learned, this new structure did nothing to alleviate the feuding; it simply made it interdepartmental rather than intradepartmental.

The major source of conflict stemmed from an inherent overlap in jurisdiction. An internal OMB memorandum described the situation by stating that the basic problem was one of two agencies "pitted against each other on the same turf with the same mission—interdicting the traffic in narcotics."[2] Customs is charged with both the protection of U.S. revenue (including the assessment and collection of tariffs on goods brought into this country) and with the interdiction of smuggled goods (including the confiscation of illicit drugs). BNDD's mission was to stop drug trafficking. Because "hard" narcotics, such as heroin, cocaine, and most marihuana and its derivatives originate outside the territorial limits of the United States, drug traffickers must "import" the contraband. Thus, virtually all internal narcotics trafficking cases, BNDD's jurisdiction, are drug-smuggling cases as well, thereby falling within Customs' jurisdiction.

Given the nature of the problem (a criminal act with both foreign and domestic elements) and given the overlapping statutory functions (allowing each agency to claim jurisdiction over the same case), the potential for duplication and conflict was obvious and often realized. Each agency sought not only the "big bust," or seizure of large quantities of narcotics, but also the apprehension of major drug traffickers, the top-echelon figures in conspiracy cases. "Nabbing the big guns" required extensive investigations, and each agency held the staunch belief that its methods of operation were far superior to the other's. Customs, armed with its unique search and seizure power,[3] tended to focus more on the border. "Cold hits," defined as those routine border inspections that uncovered narcotics, or advance intelligence supplied by Customs special agents, accounted for virtually all of Customs' narcotics discoveries. The strategy following a narcotics find varied from case to case, with agents allowing circumstances to dictate their action. Sometimes the seizure would be made immediately, and the "mule" or courier either would be arrested or, if willing, would be used as an informant who would lead the agents on to the more important drug traffickers. Other times, the mule and his load would be allowed to pass across the border untouched, and special agents would keep the individual under surveillance until the delivery of the contraband to the contact in this country.

BNDD, on the other hand, relied more heavily on a "buy and

bust" strategy that required intensive undercover work. Undercover agents would make deals with drug peddlers, either buying or selling drugs, in an attempt to acquire a broader network of informants and intelligence that would eventually lead the agent up the ladder to major drug conspiracy figures. A relationship between an undercover agent and an informant takes a long time to build and is easily ruptured. It is not surprising, therefore, that agents and their superiors have a natural tendency to guard zealously both the informant and the intelligence garnered from undercover activities. The reluctance of BNDD and Customs to share hard-earned intelligence, informants, and leads fostered competition and confusion in federal narcotics activities. The overlap in jurisdictions and the lack of any meaningful communication or cooperation between the two agencies meant that agents from both organizations could be zeroing in on the same targets or smuggling rings, communicating with the same informant, or making a buy from the same dealer—each unbeknownst to the other.

By 1972, stories began to appear in the press depicting specific examples of what was termed "destructive" conflict between BNDD and Customs. While all sides later agreed that many of the incidents reported by the press or printed in the *Congressional Record* were not accurate in all respects, the following examples serve to illustrate the potential debilitating effects of such intense bureaucratic competition:[4]

> *The most recent example (of the government trying to arrest itself) occurred at a warehouse on the West Coast, according to a BNDD source. BNDD has the place under surveillance and comes in with guns drawn to nab some heroin dealers with the goods. Customs is watching the same warehouse and thinks that those men with guns are a rival drug faction trying to heist the drugs. A scene is narrowly averted in which the incredulous heroin dealers walk out of the trap after watching two federal agencies gun each other down. . . .*
>
> *It [Customs] does keep BNDD on its toes. Recently, for instance, a BNDD undercover operative in a major city had talked his way into the confidence of some buyers and was preparing to sell them a little convoyed heroin. The BNDD man stood by sheepishly while the traffickers opened the packets, only to find that a Customs agent had autographed the shipment and put a date on it. The BNDD's clandestine network suffered a setback but the traffickers would at least realize that you can't fool Customs.*

From the Administration's point of view, the conflict generated by repeated Customs-BNDD confrontations was, in a word, "unhealthy." White House and OMB officials judged the rivalry as "wasteful, duplicative and hazardous," leading "to delay in prosecuting enforcement actions and to large expenditures of bureaucratic time and energy in resolving interagency and interdepartmental disputes."[5] In fact, the Administration believed the interagency rivalry to be so severe that it was seriously undermining President Nixon's often proclaimed "war against drugs."

Competition for Funds

In addition to the inherent overlap in jurisdiction, the unrelenting pressure to produce results for Nixon's campaign against drug abuse served to intensify the rivalry. In response to the demand for stepped-up enforcement and rehabilitation operations, old programs expanded, new programs mushroomed, and federal appropriations soared suddenly and enormously from $65 million in fiscal year 1969 to $719 million in fiscal year 1974.[6]

The massive increases in funding for drug abuse programs between 1969 and 1974 were clearly connected to President Nixon's determination to mount an effective and comprehensive attack on drugs. He tied the drug abuse problem to the law-and-order issue in the 1968 presidential election campaign and kept drugs in the limelight once he was in office. Agencies with narcotics law enforcement capabilities felt the heat from the White House as the Administration pushed for meaningful achievements and for statistics that could be released to the public as evidence of progress in the war against drugs.

The pressure to produce results that would satisfy the White House and the pressure to produce results that would qualify the agencies for an even larger slice of the appropriations pie combined to exacerbate the tensions between BNDD and Customs. Congress, while supporting the president's request for additional resources and manpower to fight drug trafficking, also insisted on concrete results to justify the ballooning budgets of agencies eager to cash in on the financial support offered for federal narcotics activities. It does not take much imagination to figure out how and why these factors added to the fuel feeding the BNDD-

Customs competition. Agencies and media alike perceived narcotics law enforcement as a sexy, political issue. The idea of agents
performing undercover activities, busting high-circle smuggling
rings, and seizing narcotics worth millions of dollars—all added
to the drama of narcotics work and enticed BNDD and Customs
to expand their activities and thus increase the potential for
confrontation.

These elements, when blended together, were enough to whet
the appetites of ambitious organizations. The tenor of agency
competition changed. No longer was it a simple matter of one
agency jousting with another over autonomy issues. More than
jurisdiction over a set of tasks was at stake now; program budgets
and organizational status were added concerns. And these concerns served as catalysts for competition. Each agency was determined to compile an outstanding narcotics enforcement record.
That meant producing the statistics needed to support performance claims and beating the rival agency to arrests and seizures.
One way to do so was to minimize communication and coordination with the other organization. Unfortunately, this could lead to
some unexpected consequences. The following cases provide good
illustrations:[7]

The "Sat-On-Citroen": *Each using its independent and uncoor-
dinated intelligence sources, both Customs narcotics agents and
agents of the Bureau of Narcotics and Dangerous Drugs learned
of the arrival at the Port of New York of a Citroen automobile
which was reportedly loaded with concealed heroin. The presence
of a large quantity of heroin was confirmed and once the car was
parked on an out-of-the-way street in the New York City area,
BNDD agents staked-out the car, seeking to arrest those who
would come to take it and its heroin cargo away. They soon
noticed that Customs agents were also "sitting-on" the Citroen.
Not wanting to lose the arrest and seizure to Customs, the BNDD
men edged a little closer to the "target." Equally anxious to chalk
up the hit to their credit, the Customs agents closed in a little
too. Apparently the stake-out became a little too obvious to the
intended recipients of the car and its heroin. The result was that
no attempt was made to pick up the car, and there were no arrests.*

A Night at the Waldorf: *A heroin trafficker-turned-informant
agreed to lead BNDD agents to higher-up traffickers in New York
City. The actual "fingering" was set up for the Waldorf Astoria
Bar in Manhattan. Customs narcotics agents already involved in*

*the case were invited along. But at the last minute, BNDD decided
to make the arrests as the "targets" were entering the establishment, without telling the Customs agents inside. The Customs
agents waited nearly all night for the targets to arrive.*

The Issue of Increasing Fragmentation

In addition to the problem of agency competition over autonomy
and funds, a second important organizational reason for reorganization was the consolidation of a highly fragmented federal
drug enforcement effort. BNDD and Customs were not the only
agencies that could claim responsibility in federal narcotics law
enforcement. Parts of the federal drug enforcement machinery
were strewn throughout the government; one OMB study counted
nine separate agencies situated in four different cabinet departments, with the major agencies concentrated in Justice and
Treasury.[8] The complement of organizations from the Justice Department included: BNDD, the Office of Drug Abuse Law Enforcement (ODALE), the Immigration and Naturalization Service
(INS), the Office of National Narcotics Intelligence (ONNI), and
the Law Enforcement Assistance Administration (LEAA). All of
these agencies played some role in drug trafficking enforcement,
and all reported directly to the Attorney General. This meant that
there was no centralized channel of communication and coordination below the top appointment in the Justice Department.

The bewildering array of bureaus armed with narcotics duties
diffused authority and diminished accountability. The urgency
with which the Nixon Administration approached the problem of
drug abuse can account for the haphazard manner in which new
agencies were created and in which existing agencies were assigned federal narcotics authority. President Nixon, in his letter
transmitting the reorganization plan to Congress, suggested that
the dispersed narcotics authority could have seriously dysfunctional effects or "serious operational and organizational short-
comings," thus necessitating the creation of a "single unified
command" to counteract the advantages "modern-day slave
traders can derive . . . from the existing organizational patch-
work."[9] The centralization of drug functions in DEA, it was hoped,
would correct such structurally related deficiencies as loss of accountability, decreased efficiency, and overlapping missions, which

at times "impeded the objective of all—interdicting illegal drug traffic."[10] Thus, the idea of consolidating narcotics functions was seized upon both as a means of improving coordination and as a means of removing duplication and waste.

The Failure of Other Attempts at Reconciliation

Another reason the proposed reorganization enjoyed such currency within the Nixon Administration in 1973 is that earlier, less drastic attempts to resolve the conflicts between BNDD and Customs had proved fruitless. These previous efforts ranged from the promulgation of formal, specific guidelines concerning each agency's responsibilities to personal intervention by the president in an effort to end the feuding between the agencies. The failure of these actions convinced the White House staff and OMB that structural deficiencies lay at the core of the problem, and that only a wholesale reorganization would put a permanent end to the conflicts.

The first attempt to arrange a truce between the two organizations involved written guidelines defining as precisely as possible the tasks and responsibilities of each agency. In a memorandum from President Nixon to Attorney General John Mitchell, dated February 5, 1970, the president endorsed those recommendations of Roy Ash's Advisory Council on Executive Organization pertaining to narcotics jurisdiction. President Nixon instructed the Attorney General and Secretary of the Treasury, John Connally, to prepare guidelines that would ensure complete and accurate implementation of the Ash proposals. These guidelines were to be submitted to the president for approval by February 15, 1973.[11]

The Ash Council recommendations designated BNDD as the lead agency in the federal government's attack on drug trafficking. In theory, this meant that BNDD was the primary representative of the United States abroad and that Customs would have no active narcotics functions overseas unless so authorized by BNDD. Customs' role would be to support BNDD in its efforts to control and eliminate illicit narcotics traffic. Although BNDD was to control all investigations within and beyond U.S. borders, the presidential directive also instructed BNDD to keep Customs informed of any investigations that might include smuggling elements. The

authority to adjudicate those disputes that could not be resolved
at the bureau level would rest with the Attorney General.[12]

Despite both the careful preparation and wording of the guidelines and what the administration called "good faith" on all sides,
the guidelines proved to be a futile attempt at reconciliation between the two organizations. Disputes continued because of am-
biguities in the language of the guidelines. For example, although
the guidelines clearly labeled BNDD as the "lead agency," they
simultaneously reinforced Customs' assertion that it had primary
jurisdiction "at ports and borders for all smuggling investigations,
including those involving narcotics, marihuana, and dangerous
drugs, except those initiated by BNDD."[13] Other qualifications of
BNDD's lead agency role left the intent of the guidelines open to
differing interpretations.[14] Consequently, the disputes continued.

The beleaguered White House staff, which took an active role
in hammering out the 1970 agreements, decided to take yet
another stab in 1971. The president personally directed the principal figures connected with the conflict—the Attorney General,
the Director of BNDD, the Secretary of the Treasury, and the
Commissioner of Customs—to "work out their disputes in the
spirit of conciliation on a case by case basis."[15] This time the Administration was urging informal cooperation, coupled with
cabinet-level mediation in the event of stalemates at lower levels.
The president's personal involvement did act as a stimulus for
resolution of certain arguments, but since it did not erase the
sources of the conflict, the flare-ups continued to occur. Bureaucratic tensions heightened again when the lines of responsibility
became blurred even further in the summer of 1972. At that time,
the Cabinet Committee on International Narcotics Control gave
Customs the green light to station more of its narcotics agents
abroad, against the advice of certain White House and OMB staff
members.[16]

In short, a variety of organizational considerations—bureaucratic competition linked to an inherent overlap in narcotics
jurisdictions, a fragmented and decentralized approach to drug
enforcement activities, the commitment of the Administration to
consolidate and unify commands in the name of efficiency and
effectiveness, and past failures at reconciling the disputes—all
acted as stimuli for a reorganization that constituted a last-ditch
attempt by the Nixon Administration to correct what it believed

to be primarily structural deficiencies in the federal drug law enforcement effort.

Other Factors Shaping the Reorganization Proposal

In addition to the organizational reasons for change, other factors also shaped the way the reorganization plan developed. For one thing, the plan had to be developed in a short period of time. The special high-level committee established by President Nixon to explore the reorganization options was not set up until December 1972. The committee had only a few months to perform its task, for the Presidential Reorganization Act of 1949—the legislation conferring reorganization authority on the president—was due to expire on April 1, 1973. Moreover, with Nixon in the White House, the likelihood of winning an extension of the reorganization authority seemed slight: Congress could be expected to balk at permitting the president to retain tools he might use to augment his powers. Thus, the committee designated to create a narcotics reorganization plan had a deadline to face—the expiration date of Nixon's reorganization authority, April 1, 1973. In effect, this meant that proposals, which in early January were as yet tentative and still in circulation for comments, had to be firmed up, refined, specified, and transformed into concrete options to be submitted to the president for final decision by, at the latest, early March 1973.[17]

The Threat of Senate Hearings

The pressure of time was further intensified when the Administration learned of the Senate Government Operations Committee's intention to open hearings in early 1973 on the BNDD-Customs dispute. This was of particular concern because Senator Abraham Ribicoff (D.–Conn.), who was about to schedule the narcotics rivalry hearings before his own subcommittee, had introduced a reorganization bill of his own on January 21, 1973. Ribicoff, too, wanted all federal activities "relating to combating traffic in illicit drugs" coordinated by, and accountable to, a single law enforcement agency.[18] But the core of Ribicoff's suggestion was to place all narcotics functions in a newly created Division of Narcotics and Dangerous Drugs in the FBI. The primary benefits of such a move, according to Ribicoff, would be to add the FBI's experience, laboratories, identification resources, and dealings with organized crime to the federal effort aimed at stemming the flow of narcotics into the country. As the senator put it: "It is an anachronism for the FBI—the nation's most esteemed, generously funded, and most resourceful law enforcement agency—not to be engaged in combating the most widespread and dangerous crime problem of our day."[19]

The grist for Senator Ribicoff's subcommittee hearings was to come from a three-month investigation of the "overlapping and disorganized federal drug enforcement efforts" conducted by his subcommittee staff and completed in March 1973. There was no doubt that Ribicoff would use the hearings as a forum through which he could attack both the fragmented federal approach to narcotics control and the Administration's poor track record in attempting to resolve the matter, while simultaneously advancing his own reorganization plan. Ribicoff came down exceptionally hard on the inability of the Administration to develop workable guidelines for BNDD and Customs, describing the documents as "more reminiscent of a cease-fire agreement between combatants than a working agreement between supposedly cooperative agents."[20]

The knowledge of imminent congressional action thus served as an impetus for those Administration officials charged with creation of a narcotics reorganization plan. There was now a need to act quickly to head off any assertions that the White House was incapable of designing a satisfactory solution to the matter, and also to ensure that the Administration's preferred course of action (assigning only a minor role to the FBI) would be realized.

The architects of Reorganization Plan No. 2 shied away from any option that would transfer narcotics functions and authority to the FBI for a couple of reasons. First, it was well known that the old-line FBI "establishment" had in the past resisted and declined the addition of narcotics duties to its array of responsibilities. FBI special-agents-in-charge, almost to a man, consistently expressed their support of J. Edgar Hoover's longstanding view that drug activities were a "nontraditional, 'dirty' business with a corruption potential which would likely taint the FBI's reputation."[21]

Second, Roy Ash, among others, worried that congressional concern over a transfer of narcotics tasks to the FBI might blossom into a major issue in the upcoming confirmation hearings on the appointment of L. Patrick Gray to head the FBI, and could have an adverse impact on Gray's chances. Ash feared, too, that even if the FBI could be persuaded to accept narcotics tasks, a "potentially serious disruption and a loss of momentum in drug enforcement" would occur owing to the "lack of FBI experience with drugs and the magnitude of necessary organizational transfers."[22] These difficulties would be compounded even further by a delay in confirming a permanent director of the FBI.

The Threat of External Studies

Yet another factor compelling the White House to forge ahead with its own plans for reorganization was the appearance of several highly critical outside studies and reports. For example, a Library of Congress study on "Federal Programs Relating to the Control of Drug Abuse" highlighted the badly fragmented nature of the federal narcotics effort and underscored the apparently haphazard structure of past responses to the drug abuse problem.

Other reports further assailed the detrimental effects of the intense bureaucratic competition between federal enforcement agencies and the inadequacy of executive branch attempts to find a lasting solution to the basic jurisdictional disputes. One General Accounting Office report, issued to Congress in December 1972, was especially critical of the continuing ambiguity of jurisdictional guidelines in the narcotics law enforcement arena. Although the GAO investigators found some evidence suggesting that cooperation and coordination between the two agencies had improved somewhat, the report concluded that the jurisdictional issues remained unresolved and that "the potential for future conflict lay simmering just below the surface."[23]

In addition, the Shafer Commission, officially known as the National Commission on Marijuana and Drug Abuse, released its second and final report, "Drug Use in America," on March 22, 1973, the same day the Administration announced Reorganization Plan No. 2. According to later congressional testimony by the group's executive director, the Commission had not been consulted about the impending organizational changes nor was it fully satisfied with the Administration's blueprint for change. The Shafer Commission also regarded persistent bureaucratic rivalry as a serious problem but expressed even greater concern over the absence of any coherent direction over the disparate federal elements involved in the containment and eventual elimination of drug abuse.

The most significant feature of the Shafer Commission's recommendations was that section urging, in effect, the creation of a "superagency" whose tasks would encompass not only law enforcement functions but treatment and rehabilitation problems as well.[24] Even though the political feasibility of creating such a "superagency" was questionable at best, the Nixon Administration did not want to be placed in the position of having actively to consider such a proposition. Thus, the White House averted any potential confrontation with the Shafer Commission over the best method for correcting deficiencies in federal drug law enforcement by unveiling and transmitting to Congress its preferred solution at the same time the Commission chose to make its final report public.

Reorganization and Political Pressures

It is clear, then, that many factors—in addition to the organizational issues examined earlier—affected the Administration officials who were charged with building a case for reorganization. The effect of these pressures and circumstances—intensified by their timing, source of origin, and the publicity accompanying their emergence—was to further solidify the White House decision to seek a full reorganization of agencies in the narcotics law enforcement arena.

It is important for understanding these events to appreciate the overwhelming importance the Nixon Administration attached to the drug abuse issue. The president and his advisers wanted to link the war on drugs to Nixon's election campaign promise that his Administration's primary domestic concern would be the maintenance of law and order. The rhetoric from the Nixon Administration repeatedly stressed the importance of battling the drug menace, for it was a key step in the direction of restoring law and order.

Thus, because the president had inexorably tied the narcotics battle to the larger issue of crime control, and because drug law enforcement was accorded top priority status in his Administration, to allow other organizations or individuals to gain credit for resolving problems in this policy arena was unthinkable and unacceptable to the Nixon White House staff. If there were deficiencies to be corrected, the White House would take the lead and, it was hoped, garner whatever political credit could be derived from taking another bold step against the drug problem. Given this attitude, it is clear that the nonstructural, political pressures outlined above were sure to be both of great concern to those in charge of reviewing the prospects for a reorganization and a decided impetus in the direction of choosing such a response to the perceived problems in this arena.

The Reorganization's Purpose: A Conspiracy Theory

The preceding pages have argued that Reorganization Plan No. 2 was crafted out of a desire to increase the efficiency and effectiveness of the federal government's drug enforcement effort. It must be noted, though, that there is another theory as to why the reorganization was devised—a conspiracy theory of sorts, advanced by Edward Jay Epstein in his book *Agency of Fear.*

Epstein's argument, simply put, is that the Nixon Administration's actions, beginning in 1972 and carried out as part of the "war on heroin," were basically a series of carefully considered steps to engineer a *coup d'etat*. The goal, in Epstein's words, was to provide the president[25]

> *with investigative agencies having the potential and the wherewithal and the personnel to assume the functions of "the Plumbers" on a far grander scale. According to the White House scenario, these new investigative functions would be legitimized by the need to eradicate the evil of drug addiction.*

Epstein's conspiracy theory rests largely on his conclusion that the narcotics "crisis" in the early 1970s was not real but invented by the Administration to use as justification for the creation of a national secret police force. To this end, domestic investigative agencies were to be set up, cloaked under the garb of a national heroin emergency, but to be used for covert missions extending well beyond those necessary for narcotics law enforcement activities.[26]

Epstein claims that the creation of the Office of Drug Abuse Law Enforcement (ODALE) and the Office of National Narcotics Intelligence (ONNI) and the reorganization leading to the birth of the new Drug Enforcement Administration were all part of a conspiracy to enhance President Nixon's power to take actions— some legal, some not—without fear of restraint or reprisal from other arms of the federal government.[27] In effect, the Nixon Administration wanted to establish a secret, unconventional, national police force that would serve the president.

This is a bold and chilling assertion, but one unsupported by the facts. Epstein claims that his research was exhaustive and meticulous, with many hours devoted to interviews and review of internal documents; but his work is marred (and his arguments undermined) by numerous errors, minor and major, in fact and interpretation.[28]

Despite what Epstein says, in the early 1970s there was in fact much evidence that the United States was facing a major drug crisis, particularly a heroin crisis. All of the statistical evidence available at the time from federal organizations and from academic and medical sources indicated the same thing: heroin usage was increasing rapidly, especially among younger persons. This usage was addictive and was substantially affecting the crime rates throughout the United States.[29] The Nixon Administration was not so politically naive as to ignore the potential benefits that could accompany a strong national campaign, or "war," against drugs. But to suggest, as Epstein does, that this crisis was artificial and concocted solely to achieve the perverted goals of an administration bent on revenge must strain the credulity of even the most ardent critics of the Nixon Administration. This allegation, however, is a key component of the conspiracy theory advanced by Epstein.

Epstein believes that the creation of DEA was basically for political purposes, fulfilling a desire on the part of the Nixon Administration to establish an independent organization controlled by the White House, free to perform whatever secret tasks were assigned to it by the Administration. He concludes that this goal would have been achieved but for the explosion of the Watergate scandal and the resistance of certain bureaucrats aware of the subversive aims of the Nixon White House.[30]

Epstein's interpretation of the events leading to the creation of DEA is, in a word, unacceptable. Epstein himself admits that during the course of his research he was presented with much evidence from individuals intimately involved in the administration of the federal narcotics program substantiating the viewpoint that DEA was devised to increase efficiency and effectiveness and to eliminate a vexing bureaucratic rivalry. He states, though, that he chose to characterize the reorganization "in terms of power rather than efficiency" because those arguments seemed the most compelling in the context of his investigation.[31]

Although Epstein did conduct an intensive investigation, his argument is porous in many places. For example, the individuals interviewed who supported the national police force theory were those who had nothing to gain from a reorganization. Men such as John Ingersoll and Eugene Rossides may have believed that the Administration had ulterior motives for their dismissal. But Epstein neglects to mention that their management track records were found lacking by responsible members of the White House staff, and that these men stood to lose the most with the implementation of Reorganization Plan No. 2. Thus, it is equally plausible to assume that their opinions concerning the motives behind the reorganization were colored somewhat by their own career disappointments.

In several places Epstein refers to the unwillingness of Congress to block the reorganization because the legislative body feared disapproving a proposal to strengthen the national attack against drugs in an election year.[32] However, 1973 was not an election year, and Congress (especially the House of Representatives) did in fact come quite close to rejecting the plan, as the following chapter will show. In addition, the Senate committee charged with reviewing the plan concluded after an independent and lengthy investigation of federal narcotics law enforcement activities that the reorganization was both necessary and urgent. The belief that some sort of action was essential to correct deficiencies in the narcotics policy arena was corroborated by other federal reports, including those prepared by the GAO, the Library of Congress, and the Shafer Commission.

But Epstein did not examine these studies, and his listing of bibliographic references suggests that he also failed to review any of the congressional documents or OMB files pertaining to Reorganization Plan No. 2. Had he done so, he might well have caught (or had more trouble ignoring) some of the inconsistencies in his argument. All of these studies, memoranda, and reports present strong evidence that Reorganization Plan No. 2 of 1973 was based on firm organizational factors. This is not to deny that political considerations played a role in the decision to reorganize the federal effort against drugs; an earlier section of this chapter has identified some of them. But these political factors are benign compared to those advanced by Epstein.

In short, the empirical evidence appears to confirm overwhelmingly the viewpoint that Reorganization Plan No. 2 was a serious, well-intentioned attempt to strengthen the federal government's narcotics law enforcement program. If one accepts this account of the reasons for the 1973 reorganization (and the evidence leads to no other acceptable conclusion), then Epstein's conspiracy theory must be viewed with considerable suspicion.

Summary

In sum, the case built in 1972–1973 for a reorganization of federal narcotics law enforcement activities rested on two different sets of stimuli—those organizational factors that seemed to preclude any solution short of reorganization, and those other (largely political) factors that prodded the Nixon White House toward a quicker and more dramatic embracing of a narcotics reorganization plan than otherwise might have occurred. Thus, the proposed realignment of narcotics jurisdictions, as viewed from the presidential perspective, would be one way to end a bureaucratic rivalry that seemed debilitating, while at the same time co-opting critics of the fragmented federal approach to narcotics law enforcement.

But whatever the perceived organizational and political merits of the reorganization idea—however strong the case for change seemed on paper—the tasks of drawing up the specifics of the plan and winning congressional approval still remained.

Endnotes

1. U.S., Congress, House, *Message from the President of the United States Transmitting Reorganization Plan No. 2 of 1973, Establishing a Drug Enforcement Administration*, H. Doc. 93–69, 93d Cong., 1st sess., 1973, pp. 183–92.
2. Internal Office of Management and Budget memorandum entitled "Drug Law Enforcement Organization," January 8, 1973.
3. Customs' search and seizure authority is unique in that it allows Customs personnel to search for people and things along the border based on reasonable rather than probable cause.
4. John Rothchild and Tom Ricketts, "The American Connection," *The Washington Monthly*, June 1972, pp. 33–44. Reprinted with permission from *The Washington Monthly*. Copyright 1972 by The Washington Monthly Co., 2712 Ontario Road, N.W., Washington, D.C. 20009.
5. Letter from Walter Minnick to Paul Levanthal, "Factual Assessment of the Customs/BNDD Dispute," June 13, 1973, p. 2.
6. Barbara Puls, *Federal Programs Relating to the Control of Drug Abuse* (Washington, D.C.: Congressional Research Service, December 7, 1972), p. 1.
7. U.S., Congress, Senate, Senator Abraham Ribicoff speaking for Reorganization of Drug Enforcement Agencies, 93d Cong., 1st sess., *Congressional Record*, February 21, 1973, pp. S2966–90.
8. Office of Management and Budget, "Federal Programs for Control of Drug Abuse, Fiscal Year 1974," undated.
9. U.S., Congress, *Message from the President*.
10. Internal Office of Management and Budget memorandum, "Drug Law Enforcement Organizations."
11. U.S., Congress, Senate, Committee on Government Operations, *Reorganization Plan No. 2 of 1973, Hearings before the Subcommittee on Reorganization, Research, and International Organizations of the Senate Committee on Government Operations*, 93d Cong., 1st sess., 1973, pp. 90–91.
12. *Ibid.*
13. *Ibid.*
14. *Ibid.* According to officials in the Office of Management and Budget, the agreement was honored only for the first few months, then ignored. Few cases were given to the Attorney General for disposal.
15. Letter from Walter Minnick to Paul Levanthal.
16. Interview with Office of Management and Budget official, August 1977.
17. In fact, by January 1973, no in-depth research had been conducted into the details of reorganization—who and how many would be transferred, what resources should go, what the effect in the field would be, etc.
18. U.S., Congress, Senator Ribicoff speaking for drug reorganization, p. S4795.
19. *Ibid.*

20. *Ibid.*, p. S4794.
21. Memorandum from Roy Ash to President Richard Nixon, "Drug Enforcement Reorganization," p. 6. Fifty-nine special-agents-in-charge were polled in 1972 on the desirability of acquiring narcotics authority. Fifty-four were opposed.
22. *Ibid.*
23. Comptroller General of the United States, *Heroin Being Smuggled into New York City Successfully*, a report to the Congress (Washington, D.C.: General Accounting Office, December 7, 1972).
24. National Commission on Marihuana and Drug Abuse, *Drug Use in America: Problem in Perspective*, 2d rept. (Washington, D.C.: U.S. Government Printing Office, March 1973).
25. Edward Jay Epstein, *Agency of Fear* (New York: G. P. Putnam's Sons, 1977), p. 8.
26. *Ibid.*, pp. 135–40, 165–77, 193–202.
27. *Ibid.*, p. 20.
28. For example, Epstein states that the hearing board set up by the task force on narcotics reorganization to elicit the opinions of those affected by Reorganization Plan No. 2 was composed of Mark Alger, Geoffrey Sheppard, and Donald Santarelli (p. 231). In fact, the third member of this board was not Santarelli but Edward Morgan. Epstein also refers to Morgan as one of Egil Krogh's "young staff assistants" on the Domestic Council; Morgan was actually Krogh's co-equal with an entirely different area of responsibility (pp. 231, 241). In another instance, Epstein notes that Roy Ash, as the director of OMB, approved a plan by Eugene Rossides to engage the IRS in narcotics investigations (p. 114). However, Ash did not join the Nixon Administration until two years later.
29. See, for example, James Q. Wilson, "The Heroin Problem," *The Public Interest*, no. 29 (Fall 1972):3–28.
30. Epstein, *Agency of Fear*, pp. 235–41, 257–61.
31. *Ibid.*, p. 307.
32. *Ibid.*, pp. 231, 251.

Chapter 6

DESIGNING THE PLAN

It was in the waning weeks of 1972 that the Nixon White House decided to take what it hoped would be the final steps in resolving the disruptive, and increasingly public, disputes among federal agencies involved in narcotics enforcement activities. The Administration, swayed by the political and organizational factors outlined in the preceding chapter, decided in late 1972 to design, and seek immediate congressional approval of, an executive reorganization plan in the hope that it would provide the solution to a vexing jurisdictional battle.

Nixon Administration officials charged with designing the reorganization were confident that they could devise a plan that would both satisfactorily resolve the issue and enjoy an easy, uneventful passage through both houses of Congress. Drug law enforcement issues and drug abuse legislation in general had enjoyed a great deal of support in the past on Capitol Hill. But as this chapter will document, Reorganization Plan No. 2 of 1973 was to encounter many hostile and traditional sources of resistance to reorganization—industry, congressional committees, clientele groups and bureaucrats—all of which at one point or another threatened the survival of the plan.

How the Administration allowed itself to be caught off-guard and how it coped with (and eventually overcame) these obstacles will be related in the following account of the birth and maturing of Reorganization Plan No. 2.

The Birth of Reorganization Plan No. 2 of 1973

In December 1972, the Nixon Administration formed a study group to evaluate the need for, and the possible structure of, a narcotics reorganization plan. The group consisted of Roy Ash, Director of OMB; Richard Kleindienst, the Attorney General; George Shultz, Secretary of the Treasury; and John Ehrlichman of the White House staff. This committee agreed that the best approach to the problem would be to designate a "working group" or task force that would undertake a review of the existing situation and develop a series of alternatives for restructuring the narcotics effort. Each member of the original committee appointed a representative to the task force. These individuals were then handed the key job of creating a reorganization scheme. The following men may be considered the chief architects of Reorganization Plan No. 2: *Mark Alger* (chief of the General Government Division of OMB, chosen by Ash); *Donald Santarelli* (Justice Department, selected by Kleindienst); *Edward Morgan* (Assistant Secretary of the Treasury for Enforcement, appointed by Shultz); and *Geoffrey Sheppard* (Domestic Council staff, representing Ehrlichman).

According to Mark Alger, the chairman of the task force, the members initiated their research by reviewing the various legal jurisdictions, past experience, and reputations of all organizations in both the Justice and Treasury Departments that in some way had a piece of narcotics law enforcement authority.[1] Because the desire to correct the fragmented approach to narcotics law enforcement was a major concern, the group conducted program reviews of each agency with an interest in drug enforcement. In addition, the task force decided that before it could devise a structure that would rationalize the organization of the drug law enforcement effort, the members of the group would have to consider exactly how and why the government monitored and controlled the movement of people and goods into the country.

One primary consideration dealt with the need to maintain border security. The task force was sensitive to the idea that any proposed shuffling of resources must be responsive not only to the needs of narcotics control but also to the problem of assuring adequate border surveillance. The U.S.-Mexico border was of particular concern because of the heavy influx of Mexicans seeking legal

—or illegal—employment in the United States. In contemplating transfers of personnel and resources to any new "lead" narcotics agency, the task force wanted to ensure that neither INS nor Customs would suffer losses that would reduce the effectiveness of their border operations.[2]

Although the task force had performance data summaries, the weight that was assigned to them is unclear. The statistics available to the study group included figures on arrests, convictions, drug seizures, and program resources for three agencies in Justice (BNDD, INS, and ODALE), and two bureaus in Treasury (Customs and IRS). All charts were up to date as of November 1, 1972. However, this author's review of internal OMB memoranda setting forth the rationale for various reorganization options, along with interviews with members of the task force, reveals that there was relatively little reliance on performance statistics in drawing up reorganization alternatives. Rather, the process of realigning narcotics functions was dominated by a desire to assign responsibilities consistent with the basic missions of the Treasury and Justice Departments.

Alternatives Explored

Working with the traditional objective of consolidating like functions and purposes under a unified command, Alger and his colleagues developed a series of possible solutions to the problem. They ranged from the option of simply maintaining the *status quo* to consolidating narcotics authority in the Law Enforcement Assistance Administration. The committee then asked Edward Morgan and Donald Santarelli to flesh out the various proposals and to catalogue the pros and cons of each alternative. Four principal alternatives emerged:[3]

Alternative 1. This option would:

1. Consolidate BNDD, the INS Border Patrol, and Customs narcotics agents in one new agency in Justice;
2. Consolidate INS inspection of persons and Customs inspection of persons and goods at ports of entry in Customs;
3. Limit INS functions to the apprehension of illegal aliens already in the country.

This first alternative appeared practical because it placed all the essential elements of drug enforcement and border control law enforcement in the Justice Department. In addition, the task force believed such an alignment of agencies would greatly streamline the existing division of responsibilities for border surveillance. Another benefit would be the provision of single-stop inspections at ports of entry, a change of great convenience to the traveling public.

The task force worried, though, that this proposal might raise serious congressional concern over the necessary changes in the functions of Customs and INS. More importantly, understandings would still have to be reached between Customs and the new Justice agency in handling narcotics enforcement matters at ports of entry, perhaps engendering a "big brother" problem.

Alternative 2.   This option would:

1. Combine the drug enforcement agencies of Justice—BNDD, ODALE, and ONNI—and research funds in the Law Enforcement Assistance Administration;
2. Transfer to Customs the INS Border Patrol and immigration functions.

The pluses of this alternative included (1) the advantage of preserving Customs' long tradition of being involved in smuggling interdiction, (2) the positive effect of one-stop service for travelers passing through ports of entry, and (3) the extended use of Customs' effective search and seizure authority.

But this proposal carried major drawbacks as well. The two most serious questions related to the expanded law enforcement role the Treasury Department would acquire and to the potentially troublesome interruption in the lines of jurisdiction over the flow of narcotics originating from overseas points (the new agency's jurisdiction) to the U.S. border (Customs' jurisdiction).

Alternative 3.   This option would:

1. Combine all Justice Department drug enforcement responsibilities and Customs narcotics agents in one new agency in Justice;
2. Augment the new agency's responsibilities by transferring to it that portion of the Customs inspection function having to do with clearance of passengers and baggage.

This arrangement would provide the consolidation of the entire job of drug enforcement and responsibility for border security involving persons (whether trafficking contraband or crossing the border illegally through a port of entry) in one organization under the authority of the attorney general. Travelers passing into the country would still be able to enjoy one-stop service, and Customs would still continue with its responsibilities for clearing cargo and collecting tariffs (which represents the bulk of the organization's revenue collections). In addition, Customs would still be responsible for the seizure of narcotics concealed in cargo which, by some counts, represented a major portion of narcotics smuggled through ports of entry.

Alternative 3 would, in effect, "gut" Customs by reassigning a large proportion of its inspection and narcotics personnel. The likelihood of winning congressional approval of such a package was slim at best, especially in view of the strong support the Customs Service enjoyed on Capitol Hill and the ruckus the agency was sure to raise over this proposal.

Alternative 4. This option would:

1. Place in the FBI all responsibility for narcotics law enforcement, research, and intelligence;
2. Consolidate the inspection of people and baggage either in Customs or in INS;
3. Place patrol of the border between ports of entry in the FBI or leave that responsibility with INS.

The possibility of handing all narcotics enforcement responsibilities to the FBI was attractive to certain members of the task force because of the opportunity it would provide for the FBI to utilize its extensive and highly developed resources and its effective intergovernmental network in attacking the narcotics problem.

The task force worried, however, that this further centralization of the federal law enforcement effort would make the Administration susceptible to charges of concentrating too much power in one agency, raising specters of a national police force. The FBI's attitude towards drug enforcement activities, a largely negative one, could create problems of integration for BNDD agents transferred to the FBI, because of the difference both in personnel systems and in qualification standards of the two bureaus. There was also a feeling that the intense interest in resources devoted to drug enforcement might well require public acknowledgment of allocation of FBI resources to various other types of enforcement efforts, notably internal security, and might create confusion regarding the overseas role of the FBI.

The Alternatives in Perspective

This preliminary array of alternatives devised by the reorganization task force raises a couple of interesting and important issues that were to affect the passage of the final plan through the legislative branch.

First, none of the proposals included the possibility of establishing Customs as the lead agency in narcotics enforcement. In fact, three of the alternatives (1, 3, and 4) recommended the removal of the narcotics investigation function from Customs. The task force considered the idea of returning full narcotics authority to Treasury a closed option, despite the acknowledgment that Treasury could never be completely closed out of narcotics activities because of its unique stature at the border, preserved by Customs' powerful search and seizure authority. One OMB official was quite blunt in his opinion as to why Customs should not be the lead agency in narcotics:[4]

> *Why would you take a step backwards? Why do you think the old Federal Bureau of Narcotics was put into Justice in 1968? Treasury couldn't handle it then. I don't know what arguments there were against the transfer of the Bureau of Narcotics to Justice in 1968, I don't know what problems were envisioned. But it just wasn't relevant in the decision-making process on Reorg. No. 2. Putting it in Customs just wasn't an option—why go back to where you know the problems are?*

Customs' loss of its high-status narcotics agents was to be cushioned somewhat in options 1 and 4 by augmenting Customs' duties at the ports with INS inspection functions and the INS personnel who carried out such tasks. The task force estimated that while approximately 650 Customs agents would be transferred to the new Justice agency, the loss would be offset by the addition of approximately 1,900 INS inspectors to the Customs inspection force. Nonetheless, as the skeletal form of a narcotics reorganization emerged, clearly a consensus had formed about the kind of role Customs would be asked to accept—a role markedly different and reduced from what it had enjoyed in the past. However, what the task force failed to realize was the length to which an executive branch agency would extend itself to protect and maintain a prestigious operation, even in the face of firm White House resolve to eliminate it.

Second, while a basic impetus for reorganization came from both the desire to end bureaucratic competition and the desire to eliminate the fragmented federal *narcotics* effort, each of the preliminary options also included provisions that would in some way affect the INS. The INS Border Patrol does routinely make narcotics seizures while patrolling between ports of entry. But INS inspectors, who constitute almost one quarter of the total INS work force, are stationed at ports of entry and rarely, if ever, stumble across narcotics cases. Yet the task force justified the inclusion of INS inspection duties in the consolidation plans because a transfer of INS inspectors to Customs would make for a more efficient system of screening passengers and baggage. The task force also argued that the transfer would tighten border security against both drug smuggling and attempted entry of illegal aliens. If both transfers were to occur—Border Patrol to Justice and INS inspectors to Treasury—INS's total work force would be cut almost in half, leaving a residual force of about 3,000 individuals to handle those internal functions retained by INS. For INS, there would be no additional functions or personnel to alleviate the loss of some 4,500 members of the organization. The failure to offer any enticements to INS would come back to haunt the Administration in the congressional hearings on Reorganization Plan No. 2, to the point of actually jeopardizing approval of the entire plan.[5]

By the end of the second week in January 1973, the task force had prepared not only firm reorganization alternatives, but also pro and con arguments that would serve as the eventual basis for decision. As indicated below, the task force members had prepared the options without having conducted any independent, in-depth studies into the level, intensity, accuracy, and impact of reported BNDD–Customs disputes, and without the benefit of any factual, empirical summaries of the potential feasibility and impact of each alternative. However, it is true that the decision to consolidate inspection functions, according to Administration witnesses, was in fact based on a 1967–1968 Bureau of the Budget study that examined procedures at ports of entry and on a "draft" GAO report then circulating on the need for single-agency management of port-of-entry inspections.[6] However, the personal knowledge and experience of executive office personnel, who in the past had repeatedly reviewed, analyzed, and advised on drug control matters, were the primary sources of information used to shape the reorganization plan.[7]

The Final Options

Prior to the scaling down of options to be presented to the president for final decision, discussion sessions were held with heads of the agencies to be affected by reorganization and with other officials actively concerned with narcotics enforcement activities.[8] After assessing the opinions and concerns of such officials as Vernon Acree, Commissioner of Customs, and John Ingersoll, Director of BNDD, three options emerged from the full committee for transmission to the president. By this point, time had become an important factor, and, as a result, the political factors outlined earlier had their largest impact on the drive for reorganization.

In fact, it was not until March 8, 1973, that President Nixon received an "action" memorandum on drug enforcement reorganization from Roy Ash. This nine-page memorandum asked the president to choose from among three options, all of which advocated some form of change in narcotics jurisdiction. The choices included:[9]

> Option 1. *There would be no realignment of responsibility between the Treasury and Justice Departments. BNDD, ONNI, and ODALE would be consolidated into one new agency reporting to one administrator in Justice. (First preference of Ken Cole; second choice of Ash and Shultz.)*

> Option 2. *Customs would acquire the INS inspection function at ports of entry, the INS Border Patrol, and all overseas drug control duties handled by BNDD. Domestic drug activities carried out by ONNI, ODALE, and BNDD would be consolidated in a single agency in Justice. (First choice of Treasury Secretary Shultz.)*

Option 3. ODALE, ONNI, BNDD, and Customs narcotics agents would all be consolidated in the Justice Department. The new agency would be assigned overseas, border, and port-of-entry drug enforcement responsibilities. Customs would maintain its inspection and border control functions (other than narcotics) and would acquire the inspection functions of INS. INS would retain its Border Patrol and internal illegal alien duties. (First choice of the Attorney General and Roy Ash.)

Roy Ash recommended presidential endorsement of option 3. Ash was convinced that this option would finally resolve the overlap in jurisdictions between BNDD and Customs, thereby eliminating the "destructive" bureaucratic rivalry. Moreover, he argued, responsibility and accountability would be lodged in one agency by consolidating drug enforcement functions in a single organization. The door would be left open for a future merger of the new agency with the FBI.

By March 15, 1973, the president had approved option 3, following the advice of his director of OMB. Option 3, once transformed into a formal organization proposal, contained these major components:

1. Created the Drug Enforcement Administration, combining ODALE, ONNI, BNDD, and Customs narcotics agents in a new agency in Justice;
2. Transferred to the Attorney General (from the Secretary of the Treasury) intelligence, investigative, and law enforcement functions relating to the suppression of illicit traffic in narcotics, dangerous drugs or marihuana. Included in the transfer were approximately 500 Customs agents (Section 1 of the plan);
3. Transferred to the Secretary of the Treasury functions vested by law in the Attorney General regarding inspection of persons and papers at ports of entry. Included in the transfer were approximately 1,000 INS inspectors (Section 2 of the plan).

On March 28, 1973, three days before his reorganization authority expired, President Nixon transmitted Reorganization Plan No. 2 of 1973 to the U.S. Congress. The plan would take effect automatically within sixty days of its submission to the legislative body unless either house of Congress passed, by a simple majority vote, a resolution disapproving reorganization.

Bureaucratic Response to Narcotics Reorganization

The task force chaired by Mark Alger held a series of meetings between January and early March 1973, to which individuals concerned with a possible realignment of narcotics authority were invited. Other than these sessions, there were no formal attempts made to solicit advice from the relevant organizations. Although Morgan and Santarelli were asked to talk over the options with representatives from their respective departments, Treasury and Justice, it is doubtful that they did more than discuss the reorganization proposals with top-level management in the principal agencies.[10]

Bureaucratic reaction to the reorganization proposals varied. BNDD, for example, had little to lose and much to gain in a proposed consolidation of its activities with those of other narcotics agencies in Justice. BNDD would finally achieve through reorganization what it had sought unsuccessfully through a variety of earlier moves—lead agency status in narcotics, an expansion of its jurisdiction, and the assurance of unhindered autonomy in narcotics (to be achieved with the dissolution of Customs' narcotics investigation and intelligence duties). The heads of ONNI and ODALE fully supported reorganization, and Myles Ambrose, who directed ODALE's campaign, was to become one of the Administration's top witnesses in the congressional reorganization hearings. John Ingersoll, Director of BNDD, did have objections to the plan because he felt that the major reason for a change, pathological bureaucratic competition, was rapidly fading as a problem. He argued that the differences between BNDD and Customs had diminished greatly with the appointment of Vernon Acree as the new commissioner of Customs in 1972. However, Ingersoll's objections carried little weight because he had fallen into disfavor with the White House staff, and the Administration planned to ease him out of the narcotics enforcement field when it came to appointing officials of the new Drug Enforcement Administration.[11]

The Immigration and Naturalization Service was the organization that stood to lose the most. As the reorganization was initially conceived, INS was in danger of being stripped of both its Border Patrol and port-of-entry inspection function—an unexpected double blow to an agency only peripherally involved in narcotics enforcement. The top officials in INS voiced their disapproval of any plan that would lead to the severing of these two responsibilities from their agency. Their main concern, as the deputy director of INS indicated to Alger's task force, was with the INS Border Patrol. Although the possible transfer of INS inspectors to Customs did not please INS management, the idea that the Border Patrol might also be placed elsewhere was viewed as a potentially devastating blow to the agency. The Border Patrol question was, in effect, the "front-office" issue with INS, since the Border Patrol unit and the agency's domestic investigation functions were seen by INS management as the principal interests of the agency. When it became clear that the task force was willing to allow INS to retain these two responsibilities, INS concern over a loss of port-of-entry inspection duties diminished. In fact, concern over the transfer of inspectors to Customs remained minimal until the INS union representatives raised vehement objections during the House of Representatives hearings of Reorganization Plan No. 2.

Customs, however, was not as willing to acquiesce to a reorganization plan that would cost the bureau close to 500 special narcotics agents from its Office of Investigation. Secretary of the Treasury, George Shultz, resisted the proposed removal of narcotics agents from Customs. In the end, he was the only member of the committee who failed to endorse the reorganization option chosen by the president. Once it became apparent that the loss of narcotics agents to DEA was inevitable, Shultz pushed for reconsideration of a reorganization plan that would include both a transfer of INS inspection functions and a transfer of INS's Border Patrol to Customs. He even captured a few moments of the president's time, right before the March 28th transmission of the plan to Congress, to plead for the Border Patrol transfer, but to no avail. However, he did elicit a promise from Roy Ash to look into the possibility of Customs' acquisition of the Border Patrol in the near future. Ash wrote:[12]

> On the Border Patrol issue, strong arguments can be made on each side. My current thinking is that it is better to leave the responsibility as is. . . . I agree that we should again review the problem prior to the end of the year. My staff will contact yours about this project once the dust settles from the current reorganization.

Former Commissioner of Customs Acree stated that he vigorously opposed the reorganization, but because it had been proposed by the president, there was little that could be done to halt it.[13] Acree did back Ingersoll's claim that cooperation and coordination between BNDD and Customs had improved since mid-1972, and he did push hard for retention of Customs narcotics agents during the meeting held by the task force. But Acree's opposition to the transfer was tempered by a couple of factors. For one thing, Acree was appointed commissioner because he was considered an Administration loyalist, who had in the past shown a willingness to cooperate with the White House.[14] Furthermore, Customs stood to gain from reorganization. By acquiring INS inspection duties, Customs' port-of-entry force would be augmented by approximately 1,900 individuals. There is little doubt, though, that Customs pushed hard for rejection of the reorganization once it reached Congress, especially once Section 2 was deleted from the plan, as we shall see.

In fact, one of the more interesting questions stemming from the process of developing the reorganization plan is whether or not the INS-to-Customs transfer was included as "compensation" for Customs for the loss of its narcotics agents. Certain Treasury officials argue that Customs was presented with INS's inspection function as a quid pro quo, in exchange for the transfer of its agents to the new Justice agency. OMB officials, however, are quick to deny the existence of any quid pro quo arrangement. They point out that the transfer of INS inspectors was a logical consolidation of tasks. They justified the inclusion by referring to two studies, one by the Bureau of the Budget and one by the General Accounting Office, both recommending the consolidation. In their opinion, the transfer would have significantly improved U.S. efforts aimed at preventing illegal immigration.

Treasury officials argue along a different track. They claim that Customs was viewed as a much more formidable opponent to reorganization than INS. They point to the great deal of support commanded by Customs on Capitol Hill, principally in the person of Tom Steed (D.–Okla.), the House Appropriations subcommittee chairman, under whose subcommittee funding for Treasury Department programs fell. These individuals insist that the INS transfer, regardless of claims that it would increase efficiency and effectiveness, was included basically to appease Customs—to "buy everyone off," to sweeten the bitter loss of 500 prestigious agents to the new DEA.

On the surface, one cannot quarrel with OMB's justification for adding Section 2 to the narcotics reorganization plan. But there is some evidence that the INS transfer was not considered an essential part of the plan. When the entire reorganization plan appeared in jeopardy of being rejected by the House of Representatives in June 1973, Roy Ash commented in a memorandum to the president:[15]

> *[The INS to Customs transfer] . . . is a sensible, but relatively minor, part of the Reorganization Plan which was included largely to "compensate" Treasury for the loss of its 500 drug agents to Justice.*

The question of whether or not there was a quid pro quo arrangement affecting the final form of the narcotics reorganization plan will be explored in greater depth when the discussion focuses on the emergence of harsh criticism of the reorganization plan before the House Committee on Government Operations.

Understanding Bureaucratic Competition

The Administration based its case for the new structural alignment on the premise that jurisdictional overlap was the root cause of a bitter and destructive bureaucratic competition and that this rivalry was corroding the effectiveness of the federal government's "war on drugs." In retrospect, however, there is some question as to how destructive this rivalry actually was.

As we have seen above, John Ingersoll was one who argued that the bureaucratic competition was not nearly as severe at the time of reorganization as others claimed. He willingly admitted that there had been a problem in the past, but that by the time the Administration had sat down to restructure the narcotics effort, the competition issue was becoming a "nonproblem." Ingersoll asserted that while the lack of clear lines demarcating the jurisdictional authority of each agency caused problems in some instances, personality clashes were responsible for exacerbating the situation. As a result, feuds escalated to the highest levels in each bureau and department as time went on, to the point where minor disputes were converted into major battles at the top echelons of government. But, according to Ingersoll, the appointment of Acree as the new head of Customs led to a marked change in attitude between BNDD and Customs, ushering in a new atmosphere of conciliation and cooperation. Both Acree and Ingersoll insisted that by the time the reorganization was drafted, the era of intense competition was on its way out.[16]

It is true that the White House viewed the competition only at its highest levels, where it affected the staff directly. The Administration and its appointed reorganization task force relied principally on second-hand accounts of the BNDD-Customs rivalry, and the reorganization task force made no effort to explore for itself how typical, how widespread the accounts of the "horror cases" were. Despite both BNDD and Customs protests that press accounts of interagency feuding often were inaccurate or blown out of proportion, the Administration, lamely admitting that in some instances facts were distorted, continued to insist that bureaucratic rivalry was having an untoward effect on drug enforcement efforts.[17] Neither the White House nor OMB conducted any in-depth, original research of their own, nor did they commission studies from others in an effort to ascertain the facts. No group actually went into the field to question those whose allegedly competitive activities were said to be having a "destructive" impact on federal narcotics programs. A good case can be made, then, that the research on interagency competition was inadequate.

In addition, no one ever asked whether or not competition is *necessarily* a bad thing. The architects of the reorganization plan simply assumed that the traditional nostrums of good management applied in this case, too—duplication, overlap, and competition naturally lead to ineffectiveness and "wasteful conflict." But at the time the bureaucratic rivalry was thought to be most destructive (from 1971 to 1973), narcotics arrests and seizures were actually at their peak.

Even if there is no sure and correct answer to the question of whether competition may, in some circumstances, be a "good thing," the fact remains that no one on the reorganization task force saw fit to explore the matter—to ask whether or not reorganization could or should eliminate agency competition.

Summary

A review of the process through which Reorganization Plan No. 2 of 1973 was created indicates that important analytical questions concerning the consequences of reorganization were never posed, either by those intimately involved in drawing up the plan, or by informed observers who testified at congressional hearings on the subject. For example, no one probed beneath the surface of the BNDD-Customs dispute. No one sought to establish what strategies the narcotics agencies employed, in order to decide if factors other than jurisdictional overlap were equally responsible for fostering bureaucratic competition; and if, in fact, this were the case, would reorganization rectify these problems once Customs agents merged with BNDD? No one asked if the tasks of narcotics agents would change with reorganization; no one asked if they *should* change. Problems with the federal narcotics enforcement effort were viewed only in terms of organizational structure. No one addressed the question of whether the methodologies and strategies that served as the foundation for the federal attack on drugs were the proper ones. These omissions were to have serious consequences for federal drug law enforcement. For example, the new Drug Enforcement Administration was to be attacked later for its lack of success in stemming drug traffic. But it was not until then that the strategies and tactics employed by the agency were called into question. It was not until three years after the birth of DEA that anyone complained about, or asked to have changed, the basic methods of narcotics enforcement.[18]

Why the right questions were not asked by those charged with the development of a narcotics reorganization plan will be the subject of a lengthy discussion later. For now, however, it is worth emphasizing that the situation was perceived simply as a matter of finding a permanent solution to a perturbing bureaucratic rivalry. Thus the process of reorganization was initiated and carried out to eliminate grounds for future competition. As a result, a plan was created without sufficient evaluation of what impact reorganization would have on the agencies and the field agents and their tasks. On paper, there existed a logical case for reorganization, particularly in traditional management objective terms. "Organizational reasons for change" served as the primary justification for structural realignment.

Unfortunately, the failure to address the question of just how things would change had important consequences for the success of Reorganization Plan No. 2.

Endnotes

1. Interview with Office of Management and Budget official, August 1977.
2. Internal Office of Management and Budget memorandum, "Drug Law Enforcement Organization," January 8, 1973.
3. *Ibid.* All details of the four alternatives and their respective pros and cons come from this memorandum.
4. Interview with Office of Management and Budget official, August 1977.
5. Congress, at the time, had either to accept or reject the reorganization plan; it could not amend it.
6. U.S., Congress, House, Committee on Government Operations, *Reorganization Plan No. 2 of 1973, Hearings before a subcommittee of the House Committee on Government Operations*, 93d Cong., 1st sess., 1973, p. 128.
7. *Ibid.*
8. *Ibid.* These officials included: V. Acree (Customs); J. Ingersoll (BNDD); R. Farrell (INS); W. Sullivan (ONNI); M. Ambrose (ODALE); P. Gray (FBI); S. Boltin (CIA); H. Peterson (Justice); and L. Goin (AID).
9. Memorandum from Roy Ash to President Richard Nixon, "Drug Enforcement Reorganization," March 8, 1973. All information relating to the options presented by Ash to the president comes from this memorandum.
10. This is according to the best recollection of two Office of Management and Budget officials involved with the reorganization. (Interviews, August 1977.)
11. Edward Jay Epstein, *Agency of Fear* (New York: G. P. Putnam's Sons, 1977), p. 231.
12. Memorandum from Roy Ash to George Shultz, Secretary of the Treasury, "Drug Reorganization," April 17, 1973, p. 1.
13. Interview with Vernon Acree, Commissioner of Customs, July 14, 1976. Acree's resignation was accepted by the Carter Administration in July 1977.
14. Epstein supports this view in *Agency of Fear*, p. 231, as did officials in both the Treasury Department and the Office of Management and Budget.
15. Memorandum from Roy Ash and Kenneth Cole, Jr. to President Richard Nixon, "Drug Enforcement Reorganization," May 23, 1973, p. 1.
16. U.S., Congress, Senate, Committee on Government Operations, *Federal Drug Enforcement, Hearings before the Permanent Subcommittee on*

Investigations of the Senate Committee on Government Operations, 94th Cong., 2d sess., 1976, part 4, p. 909.

17. This was done repeatedly, as for example in the letter from Walter Minnick to Paul Leventhal, "Factual Assessment of the Customs/BNDD Dispute," June 13, 1973.

18. The closest anyone came to urging a review of tactics and strategies used in narcotics operations was the final report of the Senate committee that held hearings on the reorganization. The report, however, was not issued until September 1973, two months after DEA began operations. See U.S., Congress, Senate, Committee on Government Operations, *Reorganization Plan No. 2 of 1973*, S. Rept. 93–00, 93d Cong., 1st sess., September 1973.

Chapter 7

WINNING CONGRESSIONAL APPROVAL

On March 28, 1973, President Nixon officially sent Reorganization Plan No. 2 to Capitol Hill. It was to lie before Congress for sixty days. In the absence of a resolution from either house of Congress disapproving the plan, it would become effective automatically at the end of that period. The Nixon White House and the architects of the reorganization were confident that the plan would encounter few, if any, obstacles in Congress. Drug law enforcement issues and drug abuse legislation in general had enjoyed a great deal of support in the past from the legislative branch. Reorganization Plan No. 2, however, was to be an exception.

The Administration anticipated no serious opposition to the reorganization, so its witnesses, led by Attorney General Richard Kleindienst, offered low-key, general defenses of the plan during the congressional hearings. The witnesses built their rationale for reorganization on the traditional tenets of good management, especially on the need to increase efficiency and effectiveness. It was left to Vernon Acree, Commissioner of Customs, to review the benefits of the changes in border inspection functions—changes that would affect both his agency and the Immigration and Naturalization Service.[1]

Conspicuously absent among the witnesses testifying in support of the reorganization plan were representatives from the management ranks of INS. But the lack of enthusiasm on the part of INS is understandable: INS was the only agency affected by the reorganization that stood to gain nothing. During the planning stages of Reorganization Plan No. 2, INS officials had protested effectively against the inclusion of an INS Border Patrol transfer to Customs, and after this victory INS management seemed to resign itself to the loss of inspectors to Customs. As a result, the White House did not push INS into publicly supporting a position with which it in fact was not pleased.

Although the Nixon Administration believed that Reorganization Plan No. 2 would be received with approval on Capitol Hill, White House officials knew of some likely sources of opposition to the plan. For instance, they anticipated minor grumblings from local INS unions. But the executive branch proponents of the reorganization expected this opposition to be simply an inconsequential inconvenience surfacing in isolated areas. Moreover, at least some OMB officials were prepared for a negative reception from Representative Tom Steed (D.–Okla.), who was expected to oppose the transfer of Customs narcotics agents to DEA. Steed was chairman of the appropriations committee charged with overseeing Treasury Department appropriations, and in the past he had been a staunch supporter of increases in Customs' budget, in some cases overriding the objections of OMB.[2] However, Administration officials believed that Steed would not be able to muster enough support to mount an effective campaign against the reorganization plan because his chosen ward, the Customs Service, stood to emerge from reorganization with a net gain of personnel, thanks to the transfer of INS inspectors to Customs. This would make it difficult for Steed and his allies to claim that the proposed changes would "gut" Customs.

Contrary to the expectations of the reorganization's early architects, opposition to the plan emerged with sufficient strength to make congressional rejection of Reorganization Plan No. 2 of 1973 a distinct possibility.

Source of Opposition: Labor Unions

Labor's unhappiness with Reorganization Plan No. 2 can be traced primarily to Section 2 of the plan, which proposed the transfer of INS inspectors and their functions to the U.S. Customs Service. The labor unions believed that implementation of Section 2 would have a largely negative, disruptive, and destructive impact on the Immigration and Naturalization Service. Labor representatives, testifying before a House subcommittee on Government Operations in early April 1973, articulated their opposition to Reorganization Plan No. 2 so forcefully and bluntly that the Administration was immediately placed on the defensive. Labor opposition to the plan, led by the American Federation of Government Employees (AFGE), the union representing INS employees, and its president, Clyde Webber, boiled down to five basic objections, all of which focused on Section 2 of the reorganization.

Weakening of Immigration Enforcement

The first objection advanced by the union was directed at the plan's potentially adverse and debilitating effects on INS's task of stemming the flow of illegal aliens into the United States from Mexico. AFGE representatives stressed that the loss of approximately 900 INS inspectors to Customs would divert valuable and already insufficient resources and manpower from INS at great cost to American workers.

Specifically, labor charged that, although the consolidation of inspection functions in Customs might increase the effectiveness of narcotics law enforcement, immigration law enforcement would suffer because Customs, more interested in narcotics control, would not give proper attention to the illegal immigration problem. AFGE argued that all the problems engendered by the flow of illegal aliens into this country would worsen and multiply if INS inspectors were transferred to Customs.

Webber and his associates acknowledged that the narcotics law enforcement problem was a serious one, but they objected to the merger of two separate issues, narcotics control and immigration inspection, in one reorganization plan. AFGE affiliates stressed that they could not find "one good reason" to disturb the existing inspection practices. They argued that instead of producing any positive effects, Section 2 would succeed only in "cannibalizing" INS by disrupting its functions and adversely affecting the morale of those remaining in the agency.[3] AFGE concluded that there was only one explanation for the Administration's insistence on including Section 2: the desire to appease Customs for the loss of 500 agents to the new Drug Enforcement Administration.

One-Stop Inspection and Cross-Training Problems

A second, more substantive and better documented objection that arose from the ranks of union opponents concerned the issue of one-stop inspections. AFGE contended that the consolidation of inspection functions in Customs would result in the implementation of "single-stop" inspections at border points of entry and that such a system had proven in the past to be both an inefficient and ineffective means of processing passengers and baggage. As defined by the labor union, the term "single-stop inspections" meant that one officer at a given port of entry would be responsible for the inspection of persons, goods, and all documents related to them.[4] Such a system would necessitate intensive cross-training both for Customs inspectors already stationed at points of entry and for those INS inspectors transferred into Customs, to ensure that each officer could competently and confidently handle the enforcement responsibilities of both immigration and customs.

At the House hearings, union representatives presented testimony from several senior INS inspectors and one Customs inspector who doubted the feasibility of carrying out a successful cross-training program. These inspectors were staunch in their beliefs that customs control and immigration control were, in fact, two distinct professions, for which no training, however extensive, could replace the years of experience necessary to carry out the responsibilities demanded of each type of inspection.[5]

Ambiguity of the Plan and the Lack of Consultation with Experts

The third major labor union objection to the proposal was based on the apparent lack of hard facts and figures on the likely consequences and effects of Reorganization Plan No. 2. AFGE charged that the plan was developed in secrecy and haste, that OMB secured no input from experts familiar with customs and immigration problems, and that neither INS nor the Department of Justice consulted the unions in advance, a courtesy or privilege to which the unions felt they were entitled under Executive Order 11491.

Particularly offensive to AFGE was the failure of the Administration to inform or consult with the union about the impending reorganization plan. The union received no word of the plan to consolidate narcotics and immigration inspection duties until a few weeks before the proposed reorganization was sent to Congress. Webber argued that this was contrary to established practice. He noted that because AFGE was the "national exclusive bargaining unit" for the Immigration and Naturalization Service, the union was entitled to consultation with the Administration regarding the changes prior to submission of the plan to Congress.[6]

The Administration, however, argued that under its interpretation of the provision of Executive Order 11491, no *advance* contact with the unions was necessary.[7] But interviews with several key White House and OMB staff members who were directly involved with creating the plan indicate that the failure to consult with AFGE and to foresee the impact of Section 2 of the reorganization plan on INS stemmed chiefly from ignorance and unfamiliarity with the executive order more than anything else. One former White House official acknowledged:[8]

> *We simply didn't anticipate any labor union opposition. Our failure to contact the unions was not a conscious decision on our part, we did not have the executive order in mind. It was simply due to our own naivete and ignorance. The unions came at us from our blind side. . . . The people who should have known to check with labor failed us. The problems the unions raised turned out to be our "Achilles heel" and they came within an ace of sinking us.*

Loss of Overtime for INS Inspectors

The labor union's fourth principal objection to Reorganization Plan No. 2 had to do with the proposal's effects on overtime for INS inspectors and INS front office personnel. AFGE contended that under the proposed plan INS employees would suffer serious pay reductions due to the loss of inspection overtime. While INS inspectors would conceivably continue to accrue overtime once transferred to Customs, union officials pointed out that the reorganization would negatively affect the pay schedules of INS personnel not regularly assigned to inspection. AFGE representatives conceded that the 1911 Overtime Act that covered Customs inspectors was potentially more remunerative than the 1931 act that covered INS inspectors. But, they argued, in practice it would make no difference because those about whom they were concerned would lose all overtime benefits as an indirect and un-anticipated consequence of the plan. The Administration, though noting that INS's overtime rules were "anachronistic regulations" in need of statutory reform, attempted to deflate the issue by stating that overtime opportunities would not be lost for those INS inspectors transferred to Customs. They argued that Customs' overtime provisions would, in fact, turn out to be even more beneficial than those of INS.[9]

Loss of Union Members

The potential loss of somewhere between 600 and 900 AFGE union members was the fifth basic issue stimulating union op-position. Although AFGE representatives did not articulate this concern during the course of their congressional testimony, cor-respondence between the Administration and the union indicated that the reduction in AFGE membership, which would accompany implementation of Reorganization Plan No. 2, was a particularly troublesome issue. The transfer of immigration inspectors to Customs would mean an unrecovered loss of membership from AFGE, an AFL-CIO affiliate, to an unaffiliated Customs union.

According to interviews with the principals assigned to adjudi-cate the union-Administration differences, AFGE was one of the fastest-growing unions among AFL-CIO affiliates. AFGE was, therefore, extremely reluctant to hand the bargaining rights of a large number of INS inspectors to a politically weak and un-affiliated union. Local AFGE union leaders were initially re-sponsible for drumming up opposition to the reorganization plan because it was at the local level where the impact of member loss would be most severe. These local union leaders made their op-position to the reorganization clear to Washington-based AFGE representatives, and they eventually mobilized national union opposition to the plan. From there, labor disapproval snow-balled, to the point where Reorganization Plan No. 2 was ear-marked as a priority vote, a must vote, on the AFL-CIO legislative agenda.

Legally, the Nixon Administration's hands were tied regarding the resolution of jurisdictional disputes among labor organiza-tions. Thus, the White House and OMB could offer little more than a promise to try, along with the Civil Service Commission, to ensure that the jurisdictional membership issue would be resolved as fairly and expeditiously as possible.

Perspectives on Labor Union Opposition

The five basic issues reviewed above constituted the core of labor union objections to the plan. Although AFGE and INS congressional witnesses were unable to produce many hard facts and figures on the adverse impact they claimed the plan would have on the Immigration Service, the fact that the Administration could provide few hard facts in defense of its position turned out to be far more damaging in the long run.

A review of the Justice Department's responses to the list of questions prepared by the AFGE lent further credence to labor's claim that the plan was prepared without a proper review of what consequences could be expected once the plan was implemented. In many cases, the Administration had to admit that as of May 1973, one month after submission of the plan to Congress, the exact number of transfers was not yet established; the specifics of the cross-training inspection program were not yet developed; and a review of the desirability of one-stop inspection systems was not yet completed. The Justice Department conceded that it was not until mid-April 1973 that OMB task forces were organized and sent into the field to acquire data concerning these matters. But the fact that the results of this research were not at hand during the congressional hearings on Reorganization Plan No. 2 helped to solidify the labor union's position and helped to fuel congressional opposition to the plan.

The labor union representing Customs, the National Customs Service Association (NCSA),[10] was quiet during the course of public and congressional debate on the reorganization plan during early spring 1973. Only one Customs representative, Francis P. Vetere, who at the time was president of the New York Council of Customs Locals, testified before the House of Representatives subcommittee. It was not until two months after the introduction of the plan to Congress, and one month after the conclusion of congressional hearings on the proposed changes, that the Customs labor union expressed serious reservations about the structural and personnel changes contained in the plan. Customs labor leaders then bitterly observed that they, too, had neither been informed of, nor consulted about, the reorganization until long after the plan was transmitted to Congress and long after the Administration had conferred with AFGE and AFL-CIO representatives.[11]

The late, yet unequivocal and forceful, opposition of Customs labor forces raises an interesting question. Why, if the union truly believed the plan to be based on faulty reasoning and to contain fatal weaknesses, did it not articulate these concerns during the course of the April and May congressional hearings on the measure, when there was still time to influence congressional action on the reorganization? One obvious answer concerns the potential addition of some 900 new members to the National Customs Service Association. After the settlement that struck Section 2 from the plan, the NCSA found itself facing a net loss of approximately 500 members, rather than a net gain of approximately 900 members—certainly a cause for union disgruntlement. Unfortunately, at least for the Customs union, the AFGE/OMB compromise was not worked out until just before a House of Representatives floor vote on a resolution to disapprove the reorganization plan. By this point, it was far too late for the NCSA to mount an effective campaign of its own against the plan.

The intensity and scope of INS labor opposition caught the Administration off guard and forced OMB and Justice Department officials to be on the defensive during the course of the House of Representatives' reorganization hearings. Even after it had become apparent that labor was extremely agitated about the plan, the Administration did not believe the unions would or could cause serious trouble. The thought never occurred to anyone that objections to the proposal could swell to the point where a House committee would issue a report recommending disapproval of the plan. But once the AFGE was able to enlist the support of its mother union, AFL-CIO, and once AFL-CIO decided to place a priority vote tag on this issue, it did become painfully clear to the Nixon Administration that labor opposition would be a major obstacle in the way of reorganization. And this opposition, coupled with an independent series of objections that arose within the House of Representatives, left the Administration nervously awaiting the final vote on a resolution to reject the reorganization plan.

Source of Opposition: Congress

The Senate

Congressional opposition to the reorganization plan surfaced only in the House of Representatives. In the Senate, the narcotics reorganization proposal encountered few problems when reviewed by Abraham Ribicoff's (D.–Conn.) subcommittee on Reorganization, Research and International Organizations (a subcommittee of the Senate's Government Operations Committee). The tenor of the Senate hearings stood in marked contrast to those in the House. Senator Ribicoff made it clear at the outset that his committee fully agreed with the Administration's argument that reorganization was the best solution to the troubles plaguing narcotics law enforcement efforts.

Labor groups largely ignored the Senate proceedings as a forum in which to express their opposition. The unions apparently preferred to concentrate their lobbying efforts and energy in only one house of Congress. This was a sensible strategy for two reasons. First, only one house of Congress needs to veto a reorganization plan to reject a proposal. And second, it was certain that support for the union position already existed in the House of Representatives. For example, Tom Steed was sure to object to the reorganization because of his staunch support of Customs in the past.

As a result of labor's decision to focus its activities only in the House of Representatives, the role of the Senate subcommittee was insignificant in terms of either endangering the plan or rescuing it from defeat. In fact, Ribicoff's subcommittee did not even issue a final report on the subject until September 1973, long after the fate of Reorganization Plan No. 2 had been decided.

The House of Representatives

Congressional opposition to Reorganization Plan No. 2 did surface in the House, however. By May 1973 the Administration realized that despite its auspicious beginnings, the plan was in danger of being rejected by the House of Representatives. On May 10, 1973, Rep. Chet Holifield's subcommittee voted 9 to 1 to endorse the reorganization plan.[12] But that action was not an accurate foreshadowing of the subsequent actions to be taken by the Committee on Government Operations. Representatives Chet Holifield and Frank Horton (R.–N.Y.) attempted to blunt labor's campaign by sending out "dear colleague" letters to their peers on the full committee urging support of the plan. Their attempts proved futile, though, as the Committee on Government Operations voted on May 22, 1973, to approve, by a 23 to 17 margin, House Resolution 382 (introduced earlier by Rep. Jerome Waldie), indicating the committee's clear-cut opposition to the plan.[13]

Congressional dissatisfaction with Reorganization Plan No. 2 was not based solely on labor's arguments, although the issues AFGE raised during the committee proceedings did lay the groundwork for a more in-depth and critical review of the plan. The objections of the Government Operations Committee boiled down to three fundamental concerns: (1) preparation of the plan by the Administration from the initial design stage to explanations of its detail during public hearings was inadequate; (2) Section 2, relating to the transfer of immigration inspectors, should not have been contained in a plan aimed primarily at more effective enforcement of drug control laws; and (3) certain parts of Section 1 left open the possibility that an excessively close and unhealthy relationship might develop between investigators in DEA and prosecutors in other units within the Justice Department. The committee concluded that too many unanswered technical and administrative questions existed to justify a recommendation favoring full House approval of the plan.

Although the primary catalyst for rejecting the plan was the intense lobbying campaign instituted by labor, once the plan reached the full committee, other factors played a role as well. For example, the promise from Roy Ash that INS cutbacks would be rescinded might well have backfired. The compromise, which was first publicized before the vote on May 17 of the full committee, rankled certain members of the committee who questioned its credibility in light of funding cutbacks already proposed by the Administration in the 1974 budget.

Another factor contributing to the ignition of the committee opposition was the strong opposition from Representative Tom Steed. Steed, the powerful and long-term benefactor of the Customs Service, produced a long list of defects in the plan. Although some of the items on Steed's list overlapped concerns raised by others, the focus of his displeasure with the plan rested chiefly on its impact on Customs. For example, Steed contended that the plan would strip Customs of manpower and resources needed for its remaining contraband and trade enforcement activities. He also worried that the reorganization would remove the checks and balances against collusion by narcotics agents in the field, thus reducing the chances of discovering and exposing corruption.[14]

A final element that influenced the Government Operations Committee to vote against the plan was the forceful and concentrated lobbying by the Customs Service, carried out behind the back of the Administration and aimed at killing the reorganization plan. Two top White House officials interviewed for this study claimed that while Customs publicly supported the plan, the leadership of Customs, in fact, did all it could to subvert the passage of the plan. One White House staff member observed:[15]

> *Customs, particularly Mike Acree, really did all it could to defeat the plan. He and others successfully influenced Shultz into refusing to use the Treasury congressional liaison system to push for the plan. They lobbied Steed and others behind our backs. They got Steed all excited by passing on all sorts of damaging, and in many instances inaccurate, information. I don't think they alone could have killed the plan but coupled with labor, it turned the full committee against us.*

The combination of intense labor lobbying, the forcefully presented opposition of Representatives Steed, Waldie, and others, and the pressure of Customs leaders objecting to the plan all proved sufficient enough to push the Government Operations Committee toward rejection of the plan. The vote of the full committee caught the Administration by surprise. In fact, the committee report recommending disapproval of the plan so jarred the Administration that many staff members who had worked on the plan assumed it was lost. However, the White House was not to give up so easily.

White House Strategy to Counteract Opposition

Although White House officials were well aware of the efforts of labor and Customs lobbying groups, they failed to entertain seriously the possibility that the committee would reject the plan. As late as May 14, 1973, the Administration was receiving assurances that, while the plan would not emerge from the Government Operations Committee with unanimous support, it was sure to be approved by a comfortable majority. For example, Richard Harkness, whose role on the reorganization team was public/press relations, wrote in mid-May that AFGE opposition to the reorganization was barely causing "ripples"—and certainly no waves—in Washington AFL-CIO circles. He stated confidently that the labor objections would not develop into a national story and therefore suggested that the White House not publicly respond to AFGE, which in his view would serve only to dignify and overemphasize union efforts. He concluded that a strong Administration stance against the unions, issued just before the full committee was to act, might result in overkill and turn out to be counterproductive.[16]

In retrospect, it seems that if the Nixon Administration had mounted a campaign against AFGE's attack on the plan, it would have had little to lose and much to gain. The committee vote was a severe blow to the promoters of Reorganization Plan No. 2. The unanticipated action of the Government Operations Committee left the Nixon White House with only ten days (at the end of which the full House of Representatives was scheduled to vote on the plan) to devise a strategy that would somehow counteract the growing opposition to the plan. A group of OMB and White House staff members had been assigned to conduct discussions with AFGE and AFL-CIO representatives. But as of May 22, 1973, the talks, though labeled constructive, had produced little in the way of a mutually satisfactory resolution to labor's objections. And because of this stalemate, certain members of the Administration were urging withdrawal or recall of the plan, rather than risk a humiliating loss on the floor of the House.

Roy Ash, working with others inside OMB, developed two options, aside from continued negotiations with labor, in search of a last-minute resolution of the OMB/union impasse. The first option recommended recall of the reorganization plan and resubmission of Section 1 of the plan as routine legislation. Secretary of the Treasury George Shultz and others argued that since the plan appeared unsalvageable, it would be politically unwise to divert scarce political capital sorely needed in other areas (such as sustaining impending vetoes) where the prospects for victory were much greater. Moreover, they contended, presidential prestige was not yet fully committed to the plan, and an unsuccessful attempt to transform a relatively minor reversal into victory might well result in a devastating "slap in the face" on an issue where the Administration had previously enjoyed strong congressional support.[17]

The second option devised by Ash's task force called for a no-holds-barred Administration effort in support of the plan. Roy Ash, Bill Timmons, Ken Cole, and Elliot Richardson all favored mounting an intensive public relations and lobbying campaign that would acquaint both Congress and the American public with the need for consolidating drug enforcement activities. In effect, they wanted to associate a vote *against* the plan with a vote *for* heroin.

The arguments for pursuing this second course of action were solid. For one thing, the plan could not be recalled legally, and thus it was doubtful that a floor vote could be avoided in any event. In addition, Ash was concerned that withdrawing the Administration's support of the plan would be interpreted as a further sign of weakness and "paralysis" of the executive branch. Fighting for the plan, even if it meant accepting defeat, made good political sense in Ash's view because it might deflect press attention from Watergate.[18]

Although it appeared in the waning days before the scheduled House vote that the Administration felt it had invested too much in Reorganization Plan No. 2 to abandon it, and was willing to launch one final effort to save it, the White House was saved from making that decision by a last-minute compromise worked out between OMB and AFGE. The salvation of the plan can be attributed to the untiring efforts of Fred Malek, the deputy director of OMB, and his task force, who together pursued doggedly a reconciliation with labor. With Representatives Horton and Holifield pushing hard for an agreement as well, Malek and his forces set up an administrative command post and dug in for one last series of discussions with labor officials over Memorial Day weekend, 1973. The outcome of the marathon bargaining sessions was a highly unusual compromise that saved the plan from defeat.

The agreement with which the Administration finally emerged

did not come easily. From the very outset, Malek and his group encountered an unwavering union demand for removal of Section 2 from the reorganization plan. After repeated consultations, AFGE's leadership presented a final offer to Malek—the Administration must not implement Section 2 of the plan and it must introduce legislation repealing that section of the plan. The Administration, faced with no other alternative, struck the deal, despite feelings in OMB that the agreement not to implement Section 2 was basically illegal. But the Administration approved the agreement, believing that it would only be a matter of days, perhaps a week, before repeal legislation could be passed by Congress, and relying on the assurance of the Justice Department that such action was not totally unprecedented.[19]

The resolution of its differences with labor by no means assured the White House of success on the House floor, however. The House vote, which had been scheduled for May 31, 1973, was pushed back to June 7, at the request of Representative Jerome Waldie, the author of the disapproval resolution passed by the committee. This time, though, the delay was to serve to the advantage of the Administration. It allowed the White House to design and implement an intense lobbying campaign. The aim was to convince the House membership that in view of labor's public withdrawal of its opposition, there was now no reason *not* to support the plan. Visits to individual members of Congress by OMB and top labor officials (including Malek and Webber) were arranged to present the Administration's strengthened case for approval of the reorganization. In addition, the White House asked Roy Ash, Elliot Richardson, and mayors and police chiefs from across the country to send out individual letters of support to key legislators, stating the urgent need for prompt approval of Reorganization Plan No. 2.[20]

Despite the frenetic and widespread activity on the part of the Administration, a straw poll of the House membership taken the morning of the scheduled vote revealed that the outcome of the plan was still doubtful. Although the understanding reached between labor and the Administration appeased the union and some House members, it apparently carried a backlash effect as well. Jerome Waldie expressed the sentiment of many of his colleagues when he attacked the OMB-AFGE agreement as a "blatant political activity" aimed at salvaging a poorly conceived proposal by circumventing the legislative process.[21]

In the end, however, the concentrated lobbying efforts of the Administration paid off. On June 7, 1973, at the end of two hours of debate, which at times was both caustic and emotional, the House of Representatives rejected the disapproval resolution, 130 to 231.[22] The Administration, recognizing that the outcome of the vote was still uncertain as of the morning of June 7, pulled out all the stops in the last few hours before the vote, enlisting the aid of such unlikely individuals as George Hoope, a congressional liaison officer in HEW, to help push for the plan. Thus the hectic, though well-structured, lobbying activities of the Administration forces, coupled with labor's public reversal of its position on the plan, succeeded in salvaging the reorganization plan from what appeared to be sure defeat. All that remained to solidify the victory was successful passage of repeal legislation that would slice Section 2 from the narcotics consolidation package, thereby honoring the Administration's commitment to AFGE.[23]

Assessing the Opposition's Impact

Labor and congressional opposition encountered by the Administration came dangerously close to sinking Reorganization Plan No. 2 of 1973. However, it is interesting to note that several OMB and Customs officials, in reviewing the course of events that took place in the spring of 1973, have concluded that the Nixon White House grossly overreacted to the pressures of the opposition. One OMB official, who was intimately involved in all phases of the reorganization, called the AFGE arrangement "the most unusual, and probably illegal," agreement he had ever encountered during his tenure in office. He claimed, as have others, that the White House overreacted to the intense pressure applied by labor, thereby escalating the chances of defeat way beyond the reality of the situation and forcing the Administration to accept a distasteful and questionable compromise.

This view, however, stands in stark contrast to that of officials who served on the White House task force seeking to mediate the AFGE-Administration differences. To these individuals, as long as Section 2 remained attached to the plan, there was not a "snowball's chance in hell," as one put it, for the reorganization to survive the final vote on the plan by the House of Representatives.[24]

Whichever version is accepted, no doubt it was the assertive objections of organized labor that forced the Administration to enter into negotiations with AFGE, the result of which was radical surgery to the structure of Reorganization Plan No. 2. Evaluating the accuracy of some of AFGE's arguments against the plan is difficult, however. Some of labor's concerns were certainly legitimate. For example, no one disputed labor's claim that the illegal alien problem was serious and growing and that what INS needed most was additional manpower and resources to cope with the increasingly severe situation.[25] But it is also obvious that certain of labor's objections were of a very parochial, self-serving nature. The potential loss of union membership, for example, and the probable loss of what, in some instances, were almost ridiculously lucrative overtime benefits were primarily in-house labor issues and certainly not the strongest points in AFGE's case against the plan.

Yet faulting the Administration for choosing to acquiesce to labor's demand that Section 2 be deleted from the plan is not that easy. At the time such a deletion appeared to be the only way to salvage the more significant portion of the reorganization scheme. The Administration's decision to accommodate the union stemmed, in a sense, from both political and organizational concerns. While all sides agreed that the architects of Reorganization Plan No. 2 did not conduct nearly as detailed a study as the problem warranted, the task force was sincere in its desire to increase and improve the operational effectiveness of the federal drug law enforcement effort. Although Section 2 of the reorganization was defended as a logical addition to the plan, the Administration's primary commitment was to correct the deficiencies in the structure of the federal attack on narcotics, next to which immigration inspection was only of peripheral concern. When it appeared that the White House was faced with the choice of either abandoning the consolidation of inspection functions or risking defeat of the entire reorganization plan, key White House officials chose the former, believing it was in the best interest of the federal narcotics effort.

However, as written correspondence among top White House officials during this time period indicates, there were political reasons as well for granting labor most of what it wanted. Roy Ash and others worried that deserting the plan, after having invested so much political capital in it, could be interpreted as a further sign of weakness on the part of an Administration already struggling to keep its head above water as a result of the Watergate scandal.

Given these political and organizational concerns, Nixon Administration officials were wary of risking a head-on collision with Congress, all for the sake of one portion of the reorganization plan that was not deemed crucial to improving the narcotics enforcement effort. One White House staff member described Section 2 as a purely tangential attachment to the plan, included chiefly as a "sop" to the Treasury, in the hopes of placating the Customs Service for the loss of its narcotics agents. Therefore, the decision promising not to implement, and to seek immediate repeal of, Section 2 was readily justified from the Administration's standpoint.

Unfortunately, once again, the Administration was forced to act in a crisis atmosphere where time was the most important element. The result was a complete lack of attention to the consequences of removing Section 2 from the overall reorganization arrangement. Although Customs' opposition and lack of cooperation was well known, neither OMB nor White House officials anticipated the continuation of Customs' hostile attitude toward the plan once it was approved. The agency, incensed already at the transfer of its top agents to DEA, could not be expected to accept graciously the snatching of the one bone that could have been thrown to it; but neither did the Administration expect the agency to refuse to cooperate with, much less to impede, the implementation of the reorganization.

Furthermore, the Nixon White House was extremely perturbed by the actions of the top executives in Customs, who repeatedly and blatantly defied orders to employ Treasury Department liaison personnel in an effort to secure congressional approval of the plan. This type of insubordination is not generally allowed, except under extreme circumstances—and this situation fell into such a category. White House officials felt they had no way of enforcing any discipline because Customs was openly refusing to obey directives from the White House. Officials were reluctant to fire top management in Customs because they feared a raking over by the press. Nor could they turn to Congress for support, because many in that body were sympathetic to Customs' concerns.

The fact that the Administration was unable either to appease Customs or to remove the unhappy and recalcitrant leaders of that agency was to have serious policy and structural consequences in the area of federal drug law enforcement. While INS and BNDD were left satisfied with the final structural arrangement of the reorganization plan, Customs was left seething. In the following months and years, much friction and rivalry was to develop between Customs and the new drug agency, DEA, and between Customs and the INS Border Patrol. With the value of hindsight, one can now criticize the Administration for including Section 2 in the first place, if only because its subsequent removal left Customs angry and determined to somehow recoup its losses.

As the last chapter pointed out, the process of drafting the narcotics reorganization plan led to the serious omission of an analytical study that would have determined exactly what impact the plan would have on the agencies involved. Similarly, the process of winning congressional approval of the plan led to a corresponding lack of in-depth analysis of how the deletion of Section 2 would affect the overall structure of the federal attack on narcotics. The resulting unanticipated policy and organizational consequences that surfaced in those agencies that received or retained narcotics functions—specifically DEA and Customs—are examined in the following two chapters.

Endnotes

1. U.S., Congress, House, Committee on Government Operations, *Reorganization Plan No. 2 of 1973, Hearings before a subcommittee of the House Committee on Government Operations*, 93d Cong., 1st sess., 1973, p. 55.
2. Interview with Office of Management and Budget official, August 1977.
3. U.S., Congress, House, *Reorganization Plan No. 2 of 1973 Hearings*, p. 81.
4. *Ibid.*, p. 83.
5. *Ibid.*, pp. 90–92.
6. *Ibid.*, p. 85.
7. *Ibid.*, p. 128.

8. Interview with former Nixon White House staff member, February 1978.

9. U.S., Congress, House, *Reorganization Plan No. 2 of 1973 Hearings*, p. 122. In fact, the Administration attempted to turn the overtime issue against the unions. Administration officials pointed out that in some cases GS-9s were making the salary of a GS-16 and that an inspector could augment his salary by $10,000 to $50,000 in one year through overtime payments.

10. This union is no longer in existence. Its representation and bargaining rights were merged into the National Treasury Employees Union.

11. U.S., Congress, House, Committee on Government Operations, *Amending Reorganization Plan No. 2 of 1973, Hearings before a Subcommittee of the House Committee on Government Operations*, 93d Cong., 1st sess., 1973, p. 19.

12. Representative Donald Fuqua (D.–Fla.) was the one subcommittee member to vote "no" on the plan. Fuqua reportedly did so to register his discontent over Congress's not having the authority to amend a presidential reorganization plan. See "Drugs: Nixon's Reorganization Plan Suffers Setback," *Congressional Quarterly Weekly Report*, May 26, 1973, pp. 1317–18.

13. *Ibid.* Two Republicans, Gude and McCloskey, voted along with the majority of the Democratic committee members. The majority of the Republicans and one Democrat, Holifield, voted to recommend approval of the plan.

14. Internal Office of Management and Budget memorandum, "Congressional Criticisms of Reorganization Plan No. 2," undated.

15. Interview with Nixon White House staff member, February 1978. This same official also stated that the White House was determined to fire Acree because of his insubordination. However, because of the pressures on the White House during the spring and summer of 1973, the Administration did not feel it could enforce any type of discipline. Thus Acree remained.

16. Memorandum from Richard Harkness to Walter Minnick, "DEA Reorganization," May 14, 1973.

17. Memorandum from Roy Ash to President Richard Nixon, "Drug Enforcement Reorganization," May 23, 1973.

18. *Ibid.*

19. American Federation of Government Employees, "Statement—AFGE Position on Reorganization Plan No. 2 of 1973," press release issued May 30, 1973.

20. Memorandum from Frederic V. Malek to Kenneth Cole, Jr., "Drug Reorganization," June 5, 1973.

21. Letter from Representative Jerome Waldie to House Colleagues, June 1, 1973.

22. U.S., Congress, House, Vote on Disapproval Resolution on Reorganization Plan No. 2 of 1973, 93d Cong., 1st sess., *Congressional Record*, June 7, 1973, pp. 18465–99. Twenty-two representatives did not register a vote.

23. Repeal of Section 2 did not come as easily as the White House had initially envisioned. While the bill encountered opposition of little significance in the House, the Senate was a different story. Senators Ribicoff, Percy, and Javits successfully delayed approval of the bill, holding it hostage for an amendment they supported. The amendment would have allowed innocent victims of federal law enforcement activities to sue the federal government for compensation. The Justice Department vigorously opposed such an amendment and a stalemate developed. It was not until the following March 1974 that the repeal legislation finally passed both houses of Congress, with a watered-down version of the Senate amendment attached. See *Congressional Quarterly Weekly Report*, March 16, 1974, pp. 699–700.
24. Interview with Nixon White House staff member, February 13, 1978.
25. In fact, a major item in the OMB/AFGE agreement bound OMB to both a review of INS resources and to an almost certain increase in INS manpower.

Chapter 8

CUSTOMS: THE UNINTENDED RESULTS OF REORGANIZATION

Every government agency has a tendency to fight for a clear and acknowledged jurisdiction over a coherent set of tasks—that is, to establish a particular domain or set of responsibilities as its own. We have seen, for example, that this desire to protect organizational autonomy was a primary cause of the repeated clashes between Customs and BNDD, with each agency determined to protect and defend its responsibilities and jurisdictions in the area of narcotics enforcement.[1]

An equally prominent tendency of organizations is to find ways of maintaining tasks that constitute an important part of the organization's ethos—the shared beliefs on the part of organization members as to the proper work and role of the organization. This inclination poses a formidable obstacle to the effective implementation of reorganization plans designed to redistribute functional responsibilities among several similar organizations. The implementation of Reorganization Plan No. 2 provides an instructive case in point: In response to the threatening losses inflicted on it by the reorganization, the U.S. Customs Service maneuvered its resources so as to remain involved in narcotics enforcement. The actions taken by Customs (and the consequences stemming from them) are also interesting and problematic for another reason; they were unintended and unanticipated by the architects of the narcotics reorganization plan.

111

Innovation and Change in the Customs Service

The U.S. Customs Service emerged from the reorganization proceedings in a disheveled, demoralized, and threatened state; it had lost 700 of its elite narcotics agents and support personnel to the new Drug Enforcement Administration. Even though they were still reeling from that loss and still smarting from OMB's capitulation to labor's demands (thus foreclosing the transfer of 900 Immigration and Naturalization Service inspectors to Customs), top executives of the Customs Service were determined to reaffirm their agency's responsibility for interdicting contraband along the nation's borders—an authority (unlike investigative responsibilities) that Customs had retained under provisions contained in the reorganization plan. Customs executives immediately began to reappraise the agency's entire organizational structure to determine how it could best improve its capability for interdicting contraband along the borders.

Not surprisingly, Customs undertook a massive overhaul of its internal operations in the wake of Reorganization Plan No. 2. The situation Customs found itself in after July 1973 was wholly conducive to *organizational innovation,* which will be defined here as either the adoption of a set of tasks new to the organization or the performance of old tasks in a fundamentally new way. Organization theorists hold that innovation is much more likely to occur in small and/or new organizations than in large, old ones, and in those situated in the private rather than the public sector.[2] Thus, while it may be less common for large, old-line agencies to change in a significant way, it does happen (as the Customs case shows), especially when two conditions are present —a sense of crisis and the availability of surplus resources.

An organization that encounters a crisis (defined here as an extreme change in conditions for which there exists no adequate, programmed response)[3] is apt to turn to innovation in response to perceived threats to its maintenance or autonomy. Unquestionably, Customs believed it was facing a crisis—namely, its potential elimination from the federal attack on narcotics. Prior to 1973, Customs' involvement in this effort had led to the development and nurturing of its narcotics enforcement activities in the Office of Investigation. Over time, this division had become the high-status unit within the agency, as a result both of the nature of its work (which many saw as "sexy" and "prestigious") and of the formidable resources and favorable publicity conferred on this division as the federal war on narcotics shifted into high gear in the early 1970s. Customs naturally viewed Reorganization Plan No. 2 as a threat both to its autonomy and to the high visibility it had enjoyed when more intimately involved in narcotics enforcement functions. In short, the reorganization presented Customs with a crisis, one response to which was organizational innovation. The comments of the Commissioner of Customs, Vernon Acree, illustrate the way agency officials viewed their situation:[4]

> *There was no sense in going into the corner like a whipped puppy with its tail between its legs after we lost out in the reorganization plan. It was a crisis and we felt we had to change to meet it. We still had the authority and responsibility for the interdiction of narcotics at our borders. So instead of sulking, we just decided to meet this problem head-on and be the best damn interdiction agency in government.*

The second factor that can act as a catalyst for bureaucratic innovation is the existence of *organizational slack,* which Richard Cyert and James March have described as the presence of surplus resources in an organization. Cyert and March argue that when an organization finds itself with time, money, and talent available to be funneled into new tasks, it will change, or else risk the loss of talented individuals.[5] In addition, Lawrence Mohr has shown that the favorable attitude of the boss or leader of an organization can be a key factor in an organization's decision to innovate.[6]

In the case of Customs, the agency did have existing surplus resources at hand, primarily in the form of talent and money. Commissioner Acree, in his testimony before Congress in the summer of 1974, recalled that in July 1973, the agency had approximately $25 million worth of capital investments committed mainly to enforcement activities along the southwest border. The transfer from Customs to DEA of 209 (out of a total of 286) narcotics agents who were stationed along this border left both a physical vacuum and the potential for underutilization of the capital assets already in place along the border (vehicles, sophisticated technological aids such as sensors and radar, and the like). Moreover, the phasing out of the agency's Sky Marshall program (instituted a couple of years earlier in an effort to deter air hijackings) provided Customs with a pool of individuals from which the agency's executives could select the brightest and most talented for new purposes. These individuals, combined with those investigative agents retained by Customs[7] and with patrol officers who were not to be affected by the reorganization plan, presented the agency with the perfect opportunity for a restructuring. A new, internal alignment of personnel would allow Customs to reassert its role in narcotics enforcement while remaining well within the sphere of jurisdiction authorized by Reorganization Plan No. 2.

In addition, the top leadership of Customs was favorably disposed to structural innovation. They saw it both as a means of maintaining the agency's involvement in the high-status arena of federal narcotics enforcement, and as a means of shoring up the demoralized attitude of Customs employees. Thus, immediately after the conclusion of the reorganization proceedings, Customs management set to work devising an internal agency reorganization. This action can be labeled an innovation not only because it was a response to a crisis, and not only because it took advantage of surplus resources, but also because it resulted in existing members of the organization performing new tasks in a fundamentally new way.

The Rejuvenation of the Customs Patrol Officers Force

Customs officials had to walk a fine line in devising an organizational response. Their task involved the establishment of a new set of internal activities that would not be in violation of Reorganization Plan No. 2. Moreover, the Customs executives had to be able to offer a credible policy rationale for the new activities; they had to be able to allay any fears on the part of the Immigration and Naturalization Service that Customs intended to challenge the INS for border patrol responsibility; and they had to be able to fend off the likely attacks from officials at the Office of Management and Budget who were sure to be suspicious of the Customs innovation.

Reviving a Border Patrol

The first problem Customs officials faced was to devise a means by which their agency could take full advantage of the ambiguous border jurisdictional assignments contained in Reorganization Plan No. 2. The plan definitely prohibited Customs' Office of Investigation from engaging in any investigative or intelligence activities related to narcotics unless specifically invited to do so by DEA. The reorganization plan, however, reserved to Customs the right to maintain a border presence. The language, which was included at the insistence of Customs officials and the Secretary of the Treasury, referred to the continuation of Customs' authority to search for and seize illegal drugs and to apprehend or detain individuals attempting to smuggle narcotics into the country "at regular inspection locations at ports of entry or anywhere along the land or water borders of the United States."[8]

After a series of high-level conferences, Customs management arrived at the consensus that the best way for the agency to capitalize on what narcotics interdiction authority it retained was to create a new division within Customs and to charge that unit with responsibility for interdicting narcotics *between* ports of entry. Customs decided that the most efficient method by which this could be accomplished (not to mention the one that would be least open to criticism and least likely to encounter an OMB order forbidding such action) was to use patrol officers from Customs' Office of Investigation. This force would be augmented by personnel from the now defunct Sky Marshall program and by the transfer of any special agents remaining in Customs who wished to remain involved in some form of narcotics enforcement work.

In effect, what Customs chose to do was to reestablish and rejuvenate a border patrol force, a unit whose history dated back to 1853. This unit had undergone numerous changes in the early decades of the twentieth century, culminating in the official disbanding of the force in 1948. The "Southwest Border Patrol," as it was called in the 1940s, was dissembled and its personnel transferred to other parts of Customs in 1948, primarily as an economy move in response to recommendations contained in a report prepared by the management consulting firm of McKinsey and Company.[9] The title of "customs patrol officers" was continued

after 1948, despite the fact that the border patrol was no longer
a distinctive entity within the agency. Instead, the customs patrol
officers (or CPOs) were placed mostly in Customs' Office of
Investigation. Their role eventually evolved into one of appren-
ticeship to the special agents, with the hope that someday these
junior officers would move up into the more elite ranks of the
special agents. Aside from backing up both special agents and
Customs inspectors at ports of entry, the patrol officers also had
responsibility for running the agency's air program, the purpose
of which was to interdict suspicious, low-flying aircraft entering
U.S. airspace from Mexico.

A Policy Rationale for the New Patrol Force

Once Customs had developed plans for its new border enforcement activities, agency officials had to be prepared to defend the
move with a persuasive policy rationale. Their argument was that
the establishment of the new division was an effort to strengthen
the agency's ability to intercept contraband, particularly along the
southwest border. Led by Commissioner Acree, Customs executives argued that the loss of some 700 agents and support personnel to DEA severely depleted the manpower force available to
Customs for interdicting narcotics and other forms of contraband
along the Mexico-U.S. border. This border, 1,900 miles long, with
varied terrain and close proximity to paved highways in desolate
sections of Texas, always had presented a difficult enforcement
problem for Customs and other agencies seeking to stem the flow
of illegal goods and persons from Mexico into the United States.
Customs officials expressed concern that illegal entries along the
southwest border would rise considerably because of the removal
of 209 narcotics agents stationed along this stretch of land. These
officials contended that once the transfer of Customs agents to
DEA was completed, the resulting gap in border enforcement
would have disastrous effects, especially in light of agency statistics showing that 80 per cent of Customs narcotics seizures
occurred between ports of entry along the Mexico-U.S. border.[10]

The rationale for an internal redistribution of agency resources
was, therefore, predicated largely on what Customs management
described as the absolute necessity of plugging the gap along the
southwest border. At the same time, Customs management acknowledged that the creation and deployment of a new Customs

border patrol, while conforming to the restrictions imposed by the reorganization plan, would also reaffirm the role the agency had played traditionally in border interdiction activities, including the interdiction of narcotics and dangerous drugs.[11] One top official in Customs emphasized that Customs sought a response that would not only deal with the problem created by the transfer of a large number of its narcotics agents, but that would also underscore Customs' conviction that OMB and the Nixon Administration had made a mistake in assigning to DEA lead agency status in narcotics enforcement. This official commented bluntly:[12]

> *The one mistake they made was trying to take Customs out of drugs. It was a good idea to try to consolidate some of the narcotics agencies, but in attempting to remove Customs completely, they left us feeling castrated. . . . But they left the door open in regard to border enforcement and we grabbed at the chance to reassert ourselves, to make it clear that we could not follow the policy of the administration. The management here perceived the plan to be ill-conceived, and we proceeded to conduct ourselves in such a way as to demonstrate to OMB and DEA that we were not fully supportive of the principles of Reorganization Plan No. 2. We decided that "by our deeds we shall be known."*

The Effect of Customs' Internal Reorganization

The new organizational structure designed by Customs dictated changes in its narcotics interdiction activities and methods. It also necessitated the development of a new set of tasks to accommodate the curtailed sphere of jurisdiction within which Customs could act.

Reorganization Plan No. 2 forbade Customs from performing any narcotics-related investigative and intelligence work. Customs officials decided, therefore, that if the agency wanted to remain significantly involved in drug enforcement (and clearly it did), it had to concentrate on seizing drugs *between* ports of entry, a task that had been neither routine nor highly developed when narcotics agents were charged with this responsibility.[13] Thus, the Customs border patrol officers were to be both adaptable and mobile, free to move along the borders between ports of entry, and free to adjust their methods of operation to the environmental characteristics of a particular location.

Customs officials knew that this new strategy would lead to a marked change in the kinds of illicit drugs that the agency would intercept. Seizures of marijuana were certain to increase; seizures of cocaine and heroin were likely to decline. The reason was simple. With drugs such as cocaine and heroin, smaller quantities successfully smuggled into the United States yield a much higher profit. Because only small quantities of cocaine and heroin need be smuggled into the country to lead to a sizable financial return, and because such amounts are more readily concealed on the body, smugglers are more apt to attempt to pass these drugs *through* ports of entry rather than *between* ports of entry.

The exact opposite is true for marijuana. For marijuana smugglers to generate a profit worthy of the risk of illicit trafficking, it is necessary to bring large amounts of the drug into the country for internal distribution. Transporting the drug in its bulky form through ports of entry is a risky endeavor (to say the least), because large vehicles are more likely to raise the suspicions of Customs inspectors. As a result, smugglers of marijuana are more apt to traverse the U.S. borders in search of locations where they can cross large vans, boats, and trucks full of bales of marijuana into the United States, with a diminished risk of detection by law enforcement officials.

Just as Customs officials expected, following the rejuvenation of the Customs patrol officers force, Customs' drug seizure statistics reflected a rise in the amount of marijuana confiscated and a corresponding decline in the amounts of heroin, cocaine, and dangerous drugs intercepted (see Table 8–1 for figures).

Internal Customs memorandums attempted to deflect any criticism or unfavorable interpretation of this turn of events by averring that marijuana smuggling had increased greatly because of the more highly organized activities of smugglers and the increasing use of illegal aircraft and "mother ships," which anchor offshore in international waters and rely on smaller vessels to ferry illicit drugs to on-shore connections. Customs officials also insisted that by 1973 existing evidence pointed to a decline in the flow of heroin into the United States, although there was also evidence that the amount of cocaine entering the United States was rising.[14]

Another factor led Customs to predict a shift in its narcotics seizure statistics. Reorganization Plan No. 2 prohibited Customs from conducting any drug investigations and from gathering any independent intelligence for the sole purpose of initiating in-

Table 8–1   Comparative Drug Seizure Statistics for Calendar Years 1973 and 1974

	1973	1974	Percentage of Change
Heroin			
Number of seizures	516	419	−18.8
Quantity (pounds)	203	82	−60.6
Opium			
Number of seizures	91	71	−22.0
Quantity (pounds)	116	27	−76.7
Cocaine			
Number of seizures	1,113	936	−15.9
Quantity (pounds)	856	629	−26.5
Other narcotics			
Number of seizures	326	170	−47.9
Quantity (pounds)	123	289	+135.0
Marijuana			
Number of seizures	10,356	14,000	+35.2
Quantity (pounds)	399,529	530,073	+32.7
Hashish			
Number of seizures	3,695	3,500	−5.3
Quantity (pounds)	7,235	6,161	−14.8
Dangerous drugs			
Number of seizures	2,377	2,345	−1.3
Quantity (5 gram units)	31,111,656	9,414,972	−69.7

Source: Figures compiled by the Department of Treasury, U.S. Customs Service, Office of Enforcement Support, June 1975.

vestigations that might lead to the arrest of individuals involved in narcotics smuggling. Experience had taught those involved in narcotics enforcement activities that without the aid of intelligence or advance information, nabbing cocaine and heroin smugglers passing through ports of entry with traditionally heavy traffic patterns is difficult. With intelligence no longer emanating from its own Office of Investigation, Customs would have to rely principally on the receipt of leads from DEA;[15] considering the lack of cooperation and the strained relationship between the two agencies, it was doubtful that Customs would acquire enough intelligence from DEA to maintain its previous cocaine and heroin seizure records.[16]

In short, the organizational innovation devised and implemented by Customs had two general results. First, it enabled Customs to achieve its goal of retaining an active and significant role in the federal attack on narcotics. Second, it led to a number of out-comes unintended by those who had designed Reorganization Plan No. 2, including a still-prominent role for Customs in this policy arena, and a substantial increase in Customs' marijuana seizures. The Customs innovations also led, as we shall see below, to new problems of conflict and rivalry between Customs and the Immigration and Naturalization Service (which had its own border patrol force) and to continued failures of coordination and cooperation between Customs and DEA.

The Unintended Consequences of Reorganization Plan No. 2

The 1973 reorganization was drafted and implemented with the hope of enhancing the management and performance of federal narcotics law enforcement activities. The architects of the plan advanced it with a host of "good government" nostrums, including the need to eliminate duplication and overlap and to reduce pathological bureaucratic rivalries. It is especially ironic, then, that the Customs Service's innovative reinstitution and strength-ening of its presence along the borders (a move unintended and unanticipated by the architects of Reorganization Plan No. 2) caused new problems akin to those the reorganization was in-tended to eliminate.

Conflicts with INS

The Customs innovation caused new conflicts between Customs and the Immigration and Naturalization Service over which agency should have lead status in border law enforcement ac-tivities. Customs and Treasury officials clearly believed that Cus-toms would be the logical place within which to consolidate border functions vested in other departments and agencies, espe-cially those functions performed by INS at and between ports of entry. These Customs officials urged the Office of Management and Budget to review the splintered ports-of-entry and border search responsibilities of various federal agencies. Customs wanted OMB to determine if a consolidation of these activities would be in the best interest of increased efficiency and effectiveness. Not surprisingly, some OMB officials regarded Customs' request with suspicion; they believed that Customs' deployment of a new border force was a move intended to solidify the agency's position along the borders, thereby pushing OMB into the position of having to designate Customs as the new lead agency for all border law enforcement activities.[17]

Despite these concerns, OMB did undertake a study, beginning in 1973, of federal law enforcement activities along the southwest border. Interestingly, the date of commencement of the OMB review coincided with the start of congressional hearings on Customs' request for supplemental appropriations to help with the implementation of changes in the structure of its work force. This point is worthy of note because of the conclusions drawn by the OMB study. Much to Customs' surprise and dismay, OMB recommended both that INS be tapped as the single agency in charge of routine patrols along the land border between ports and that the deployment of Customs patrol officers to ports of entry be curtailed.[18]

This time, although OMB was not drafting a formal reorganization plan (it could not do so because presidential reorganization authority had expired April 1, 1973, and was not yet renewed by Congress), an intensive six-month study was conducted, task forces were sent into the field prior to the drawing up of options, and the relevant agencies, INS and Customs, were asked to submit to OMB their respective proposals for consolidation of border patrol functions before OMB was to make its final decision. Not surprisingly, the Department of Justice issued a lengthy report urging recognition of INS (a Justice agency) as the lead unit for all land patrol operations between ports of entry.[19] In direct contrast, the U.S. Customs Service analysis proposed that Customs have primary responsibility for border area enforcement and that INS patrol officers be withdrawn from the border and stationed only at interior points.[20]

The plan upon which OMB finally settled was set forth in two letters issued June 5, 1974, and forwarded to the Attorney General and to the Secretary of the Treasury. The letters were not considered formal documents, and because OMB officials believed they were not changing fundamentally the functions of INS or Customs, Congress was not informed of the plan. The new OMB "management strategy," as it was called, stipulated that responsibility for law enforcement along the Mexico-U.S. border be placed in the hands of a single agency, INS. In practice, the single-agency concept would confer even greater responsibility on INS than the Justice Department had envisioned. Under the OMB plan, Customs patrol officers were to be withdrawn from the border, leaving INS with jurisdiction for the interdiction of both people and goods between ports of entry, effectively eliminating the newly reactivated Customs patrol force, a change not suggested by the Justice Department.[21]

Whether OMB's decision to grant INS lead agency status and other responsibilities was grounded on principles of "good management" or merely an attempt to retaliate against Customs for that agency's actions preceding, and subsequent to, the implementation of Reorganization Plan No. 2, is open to conjecture.[22] The more important point is that OMB was not afforded the opportunity to implement its decisions. When members of the House Committee on Government Operations received wind of the plan (purportedly from sources inside Customs), they immediately announced that the committee would hold hearings on the plan.

The congressional committee, while acknowledging that it made little sense to have two different agencies performing similar border patrol functions, concluded that both INS and Customs had separate statutory authority that justified the presence of both agencies along the border. Moreover, the committee determined that OMB was operating under questionable legal status "in attempting to promulgate without congressional sanction, a plan for single-agency management in southwestern border areas and functions."[23] Acting upon these considerations, the House of Representatives went on record against the OMB proposal, and by a vote of 283–100 adopted an amendment to HR 15544 forbidding any use of funds to carry out a transfer of Customs border interdiction duties to INS.[24]

The actions of the House of Representatives effectively eliminated any hope OMB had of achieving the goal of single-agency management of border patrol duties. However, the desirability of consolidating border enforcement responsibilities remains an issue even today. The problems of duplication, overlap, and lack of coordination between Customs and INS along the southwest border of the United States, although not pressing issues demanding immediate attention, still raise frequent calls for a single border management agency.

The Carter Administration, for example, drafted a reorganization plan in 1978 that sought to rectify the problem of conflict and overlap between Customs patrol officers and the INS Border Patrol. Originally there were three options under consideration: the first would simply beef up both Customs and INS resources along the Mexico-U.S. border; the second would combine the *patrol* functions of the two agencies in one department (either Justice or Treasury) and transfer all *inspection* duties to the other; the third would create a border management agency in either Treasury or Justice and assign to it both the inspection and patrol functions.[25]

The version approved by the Carter Administration proposed the creation of a new Border Management Service. Under this arrangement, the INS Border Patrol would have merged with the U.S. Customs Service in the Treasury Department. This move would have been accompanied by the transfer of visa-control functions from the State Department to INS. But vigorous opposition to the reorganization plan—emanating mainly from the key congressional committees with oversight responsibility over these agencies, from organized labor, and from Hispanic groups—effectively scuttled the plan.[26]

Persistent Problems with DEA

Just as the new conflicts between Customs and INS were unanticipated by the architects of Reorganization Plan No. 2, so also were the persistent failures to achieve coordination and cooperation between Customs and the new Drug Enforcement Administration. From the very outset, Customs' stance toward DEA was one of obstruction and obstinance. By August 1973, OMB was describing the relations between DEA and Customs as "poor and deteriorating," with "very little communication between the two agencies and only minimal interest in cooperation or accommodation."[27] Part of the problem was that DEA still did not have a permanent administrator at that point. OMB also apportioned much of the blame on the shoulders of Customs management. Indeed, Customs officials admitted that Customs' quarrelsome and uncooperative posture, on major and minor issues, was a deliberate strategy on the part of Customs.[28] One former Customs official noted that his old agency's harassment of DEA was often unethical or questionable, if not illegal: "We wanted to slam

DEA so bad that we would even fool with or manipulate statistics, keeping some back, making up others, fouling up their data; it was almost criminal. And we were obsessed with it."[29]

Not surprisingly, OMB encountered great difficulty in resolving issues that ranged from Customs' failure to grant search and seizure authority to DEA agents stationed along the border, to disagreements over the procedures to be used in handling Customs drug seizures, to the inability of the two agencies to agree on guidelines governing the passage of drugs through Customs inspection points for investigative purposes.[30]

Perhaps the most frustrating aspect of the early clashes between DEA and Customs was that the old battle lines between BNDD and Customs, which the Administration had hoped to erase by means of Reorganization Plan No. 2, were being redrawn. Customs, by its internal reorganization and its stubbornness at the negotiating table, demonstrated openly both its refusal to fade into the background of federal drug enforcement activities and its hostility toward DEA. Knowing full well that Customs was reluctant to do anything that might make DEA a success, DEA executives countered by directing (as one observer put it) "an aggressive effort to *monopolize* narcotics enforcement; the door would not be opened even a crack to let Customs assist in narcotics control efforts."[31]

The failure of OMB to resolve the impasses between DEA and Customs led to a situation very familiar to White House officials (but not expected to be a consequence of Reorganization Plan No. 2): top leaders in the Treasury and Justice Departments were forced to enter the disputes, as they had during the course of earlier conflicts between Customs and BNDD, in an effort to arrive at some mutually satisfactory compromise (or at least to paper over the differences). This form of confrontation was precisely what the architects of Reorganization Plan No. 2 had hoped to eliminate in 1973.

Later Developments

With the advent of Ronald Reagan's Administration in January 1981, the whole issue of reorganization and reassignment of narcotics jurisdictions once again emerged, as the new Administration showed a desire to do something about the problem of illegal narcotics trafficking. Customs clearly viewed the renewed interest in narcotics as an opportunity to recoup the losses it suffered in 1973. While rumors abounded in early spring 1981 about a potential dismantling of DEA and a transferral of its duties and personnel to the Federal Bureau of Investigation (FBI), Customs officials were hard at work lobbying the new administration for a reinstatement of jurisdiction for drug investigations.

Customs' efforts were rewarded when Donald T. Regan, Secretary of the Treasury, forwarded to Edwin Meese, President Reagan's senior policy adviser, a memorandum urging approval of a realignment of narcotics jurisdictions. Regan also argued that Customs should be allowed to regain a major role in this policy arena. The memorandum was blunt and clear in its reference to the 1973 narcotics agency reorganization; it recommended that "appropriate steps be taken to undo the effects of Reorganization Plan No. 2 of 1973."[32] The authors of the memorandum reasoned that the 1973 reorganization had not been successful in attacking the many facets of drug trafficking because, as they put it,[33]

the job is simply too big for a single mission agency like DEA. . . . A single mission agency tends to be jealous of its jurisdiction, inhibiting intelligence sharing and investigative cooperation, and thereby discouraging participation by other agencies. . . . [This] approach may be inherently unworkable because such an agency depends upon the continuation of the problem for its own survival.

In the years since the implementation of Reorganization Plan No. 2, the Customs Service has grudgingly clung to its view that the agency was wronged by the architects of the 1973 reorganization. Customs officials have repeatedly tried to undermine DEA's work. It is no surprise to anyone familiar with the rocky political terrain of this policy arena that Customs would try further to discredit DEA and vigorously press its case to win back the drug enforcement authority it once had. But Customs was to lose in this latest round as well, when the Reagan Administration decided in early 1982 to assign the FBI concurrent jurisdiction, with the DEA, over narcotics enforcement.

The Unintended Consequences of Reorganization: Were They Avoidable?

The basic purpose of the reorganization was the consolidation of federal narcotics activities in one lead agency. Because Customs was not chosen as that agency, an accompanying decline in the responsibilities and duties of Customs in this policy arena should have taken place. However, the distinction between interdiction and investigation—the former to be retained by Customs and the latter to be the province of DEA—was not spelled out precisely and unambiguously in the legislation. Customs, therefore, was afforded the opportunity to stay much moré involved in the federal attack on narcotics than the reorganization's architects had envisioned.

Customs did not take long to reassert its authority in the narcotics enforcement field, doing so primarily by reactivating its uniformed force of patrol officers along the southwest border. This move, coupled with the agency's uncompromising (sometimes hostile and obstructive) attitude toward DEA, caught everyone concerned off guard. For example, OMB certainly did not anticipate Customs' forceful reentry into the narcotics arena. But the behavior of Customs (and the consequences of the agency's actions) can hardly be blamed on OMB. After all, OMB officials fully expected (and reasonably so) that Customs would accept the conditions of the president's reorganization plan. Customs, however, was not willing to play the part of the loyal soldier.

Had OBM known in advance of Customs' plans, and had OMB been successful in impeding the implementation of those plans, perhaps the ensuing conflicts could have been avoided. Yet even if OMB had anticipated Customs' actions, whether it could have stopped the agency from behaving as it did is uncertain. After all, as OMB learned in the spring of 1974, Congress was in full agreement with Customs' stance that the agency had a statutory right to maintain a force along the U.S. borders. In fact, the very language drafted by OMB and contained in Reorganization Plan No. 2 (originally included to appease Customs) was used to back up this opinion.

OMB's belated decision to merge border patrol functions into one agency had a good deal of merit: It was a rational attempt to resolve the problems of conflict and overlap between INS and Customs. The problem of overlapping border functions, exacerbated by the rejuvenation of the Customs patrol force, still warrants attention today. But given the statutory authority of each agency, and given the determination of each to hold on to what it now possesses, a long and bitter battle will likely erupt whenever a new solution is again proposed.[34] Furthermore, Customs' lobbying of the Reagan Administration clearly indicates that Customs has yet to accept the losses it suffered in 1973.

Moreover, even if OMB and Nixon Administration officials had specific, advance knowledge of Customs' desire to reenter the narcotics field, it is uncertain that they could have prevented the agency from doing so. It is true that the reorganization plan prohibited Customs' Office of Investigation from engaging in any form of investigative activity related to narcotics. But the reorganization plan also specified that Customs was to retain interdiction duties, toward which the tasks of the Customs patrol force were then tailored. As DEA has labored to point out on numerous occasions, the theoretically distinct functions of patrol and investigation can come into conflict and competition with one another. The interdiction of narcotics can provide unexpected opportunities for patrol organizations to engage in investigative work; that may in turn lead to a decrease in the supply of leads to the investigative unit and a corresponding decrease in actual patrol efforts. Similarly, there is a fair probability that both patrol and investigative officers may unknowingly be working on the same case or that a patrol force may flood investigators with what it feels are good leads, thereby inhibiting investigators from pursuing attractive leads of their own.[35] Given these possibilities, that conflict and competition developed between Customs and DEA is not surprising.

Moreover, even if Customs had not reactivated its patrol unit, difficulties between DEA and Customs might well have ensued anyway. There is no question that DEA perceived Customs as "the enemy" that would be out to thwart the success of the new drug agency. Therefore, DEA was not inclined toward any generosity in its dealings with Customs and viewed any Customs narcotics enforcement endeavors with decided suspicion. In fact, in early 1975 DEA was concerned about reports from what it called "reliable sources" indicating that Customs had a "secret plan" ready to undo the major thrusts of Reorganization Plan No. 2 by means of legislation and to regain for itself a major role in narcotics enforcement.[36]

In the final analysis, the consequences of the reorganization plan as they affected Customs' relationship with DEA, and possibly Customs' relationship with INS, could not have been avoided even if the actions of Customs had been anticipated by White House officials. As Mark Moore has theorized, the nature of the tasks of the relevant organizations virtually dictated the development of conflicts among the relevant agencies. Each organization followed a certain set of procedures, each was limited by a fixed allocation of resources, and each had a specific sense of how it should go about carrying out its mission, thereby limiting the manner in which each structured and performed its tasks.[37] It was inevitable that conflicts would emerge: each organization developed a specialization in particular enforcement tactics, each organization was convinced its style was better, and each had the jurisdiction to do what it was doing. Even a massive administrative reshuffling can accomplish little under such circumstances.

Endnotes

1. See Chapter 5 for the reasons behind the disputes.
2. Private organizations are likely to innovate more frequently because they face more challenges to their survival and because they have more control over factors of production than do public organizations.
3. See James Q. Wilson, "Innovation in Organizations: Notes Toward a Theory," in James D. Thompson, ed., *Approaches to Organizational Design* (Pittsburgh: University of Pittsburgh Press, 1966), pp. 193–218.
4. Interview with Customs official, July 1976.
5. Richard Cyert and James March, *A Behavioral Theory of the Firm* (Englewood Cliffs, N.J.: Prentice-Hall, 1963), pp. 36–38, 278–79.
6. Lawrence B. Mohr, "Determinants of Innovation in Organizations," in Lloyd A. Rowe and William B. Boise, eds., *Organization and Managerial Innovation* (Pacific Palisades, Calif.: Goodyear Publishing Co., 1973), pp. 49–75.
7. The agents transferred to DEA were those for whom 50 per cent or more of their time was spent on narcotics investigations.
8. From Section 1 of the reorganization plan in: U.S., Congress, House, *Message from the President of the United States Transmitting Reor-*

ganization Plan No. 2 of 1973, Establishing a Drug Enforcement Administration, H. Doc. 93–69, 93d Cong., 1st sess., 1973, p. 190.

9. McKinsey and Company, Inc., "Management Survey of the Bureau of Customs," Chap. VIII, January 1948 (typewritten).

10. U.S., Congress, House, Committee on Government Operations, *Law Enforcement on the Southwest Border, Hearings before a Subcommittee of the House Committee on Government Operations*, 93d Cong., 2d sess., 1974, pp. 106–07.

11. Department of the Treasury, U.S. Customs Service, "Integrated Interdiction Program: Briefing Document," June 1975 (typewritten), p. 1.

12. Interview with Customs official, June 1976.

13. Interviews with narcotics agents indicated that the investigative and intelligence work was the "sexy" aspect of their narcotics duties; interdiction was a secondary concern, although a task that provided leads for investigative activities. However, interdiction, in and of itself, was not regarded as the most significant work of the agents.

14. Department of the Treasury, U.S. Customs Service, "Integrated Interdiction Program," pp. 2–3. Figures compiled by Customs showed a sharp increase in the number of cocaine seizures and an increase in the quantities of cocaine confiscated between fiscal year 1972 and fiscal year 1973.

15. Customs did have a communications system known as "TECS," which was being updated and expanded to provide instant access to centralized enforcement files.

16. As of May 1, 1975, Customs was still complaining that it was receiving virtually no data or advance intelligence from DEA, although Customs generally requested such on the average of twice per month.

17. Interviews with Office of Management and Budget officials, June 1976 and August 1976.

18. Office of Management and Budget, "U.S. Border Patrol Operating Plan for Detection and Interdiction of Illegal Aliens and Drugs," July 11, 1974 (typewritten).

19. U.S. Department of Justice, "A Secure Border: An Analysis of Issues Affecting the U.S. Department of Justice," March 4, 1974 (typewritten). This study, while favoring INS as the lead agency, did acknowledge that Customs had a legitimate role in border enforcement. Therefore, it did not recommend a takeover of any Customs functions, but rather recommended an official pronouncement of INS as the lead agency and the development of formal agreements identifying each agency's jurisdiction and delineating the working relationships between INS, DEA, and Customs.

20. The Treasury Department's proposal went much further than that of the Justice Department in that it proposed realigning the INS Border Patrol, arguing that INS was not "equipped" for contraband interdiction and therefore would not be effective in this pursuit. See Department of the Treasury, U.S. Customs Service, "A Balanced Program to Combat Smuggling and to Integrate Customs Enforcement Efforts," November

27, 1973 (typewritten) and Department of the Treasury, U.S. Customs Service, "A Study of the Impact of Marihuana Smuggling," May 1974 (typewritten).

21. The Justice Department proposal did not contain any plans for the removal of the Customs force from the border. It suggested only that INS be designated the lead agency in charge of supervising and coordinating the activities of both its own Border Patrol and Customs' patrol force.

22. Several Customs officials have expressed the belief that this was in fact the case. For a recitation of the reasons behind OMB's decision, see U.S., Congress, *Law Enforcement on the Southwest Border*, H. Rept. 93–1630, pp. 3–5.

23. *Ibid.*, pp. 28–30.

24. *Congressional Quarterly Almanac*, 1974, pp. 78–79. The amendment was attached to the 1974 appropriations bill on June 25, 1974.

25. *The Washington Post,* 7 April 1978, p. C 15.

26. *The New York Times*, 26 July 1978, P. A 9.

27. Memorandum from Walter Minnick to Roy Ash entitled "Unresolved Drug Reorganization Issues," August 15, 1973.

28. Interview with Customs official, June 1976.

29. Interview with former Customs official, July 1981.

30. Memorandum from Walter Minnick to Roy Ash, "Unresolved Drug Reorganization Issues."

31. Mark H. Moore, "Reorganization Plan #2 Reviewed: Problems in Implementing a Strategy to Reduce the Supply of Drugs to Illicit Markets in the United States," *Public Policy* 26 (Spring 1978):250. Moore goes on to state that former Customs officials, now in DEA, advised DEA officials to take the "hard line" against Customs.

32. Memorandum for Edwin Meese, III, counselor to the President, from Donald T. Regan, Secretary of the Treasury, p. 5.

33. *Ibid.*, p. 4.

34. This is an old problem that dates back to 1943 when management consultants suggested a merger of the functions of the various agencies operating along the border.

35. Memorandum from John Bartels to Laurence J. Silberman, deputy attorney general, entitled "Agenda of Unresolved Issues between Customs and DEA," December 4, 1974.

36. Internal U.S. Justice Department memorandum, untitled, Winter 1975 (typewritten), pp. 2, 25. Despite the worries of DEA, nothing of this sort ever evolved in Congress.

37. Mark H. Moore, "Reorganization Plan #2 Reviewed: Problems in Implementing a Strategy to Reduce the Supply of Drugs to Illicit Markets in the United States," unpublished manuscript, December 31, 1975, pp. 1, 10. (This was an earlier version of the article written by Moore of the same title cited above.)

Chapter 9

DEA: THE FAILURE OF REORGANIZATION

The U.S. Drug Enforcement Administration (DEA), created in 1973 by Reorganization Plan No. 2, stands as testimony to the changeability and adaptability of the federal executive branch. Nixon Administration officials—convinced of the need for a single, lead agency in federal drug law enforcement activities—created DEA out of four units: the Bureau of Narcotics and Dangerous Drugs (BNDD), the Office of Drug Abuse and Law Enforcement (ODALE), the Office of National Narcotics Intelligence (ONNI), and the contingent of 700 narcotics agents and support personnel transferred from the Customs Service. In short, this was a sweeping set of changes, carried out amidst great expectations for its likely success in strengthening the federal attack on drugs.

Yet eight years later, in 1981, DEA stands as testimony to the failure of this and other federal executive reorganizations. Despite the changes implemented in 1973, the federal government's efforts to stem the traffic in illicit drugs are the target of serious criticisms. The general consensus inside governmental circles and among attentive outside observers is that DEA's performance has fallen far short of the expectations of the agency's architects. In fact, in 1981, DEA was considered so unsuccessful that calls emerged anew for a reorganization of federal narcotics activities.

The explanations for this disappointing outcome illustrate several of the fundamental difficulties common to many federal executive reorganizations. First, and probably most important, many of the problems encountered by DEA can be traced to the inadequate analysis of federal drug law enforcement procedures

131

and tasks at the time of the 1973 reorganization. As is often the case with executive reorganizers, the designers of DEA failed to undertake a serious, detailed analysis of the strategies and tactics employed by the four agencies to be consolidated into the new DEA or those to be adopted by this new agency. By failing to study and understand the strategies and tasks of operators performing drug enforcement tasks in the field, the reorganization's Washington-based architects failed to perceive what could and what could not be changed by means of a reorganization that concerned itself solely with a redistribution of personnel and authority. The DEA experience illustrates an important principle of executive reorganization: for a reorganization to have a discernible impact on the output of an agency, it must somehow affect or alter the basic tasks of operating-level personnel.

Second, as is so often the case with reorganizations of federal agencies, the new DEA suffered from instability and inconsistency in its top management ranks. Finally, like many offspring of reorganizations, the new Drug Enforcement Administration was born into an unreceptive and occasionally hostile environment, with other agencies (in this case, Customs) eager to undermine its effectiveness, and with Congress poised for attack should the agency's performance not satisfy congressional expectations.

DEA's Methods of Operation

Those who were responsible for the creation of DEA believed that the new agency would select and refine the best of the assorted operating methods and enforcement strategies of the various agencies consolidated to form DEA. These approaches varied greatly. For example, the Bureau of Narcotics and Dangerous Drugs (BNDD) defined its primary objective as reducing the availability of narcotics in the United States by focusing on the identification and immobilization of major domestic and international rings engaged in illicit drug trafficking. The chief strategy by which BNDD sought to achieve its goal was the assignment of BNDD agents to undercover work. Agents dressed and lived as narcotics users and traffickers in the hope of infiltrating major narcotics systems. A key factor aiding the agents in their attempts to gain the confidence of drug dealers and enter their organizations was the availability of funds to be used to purchase information from informants and to purchase evidence in the form of illegal drugs. Ideally, the expenditure of these funds would allow a federal narcotics agent to "buy into" or penetrate a drug ring, from which point the agent could work progressively up the ladder in an effort to implicate the major suppliers and financers of narcotics trafficking organizations.

The Customs Service, on the other hand, relied primarily on the "convoy" as the focal point of its drug enforcement activities. Under the convoy approach, Customs agents would allow narcotics traffickers to pass through ports of entry without letting the suspects know they were under surveillance. The investigators would then follow the couriers and their goods to their next contact in the United States. The Customs agents would continue this method until they could make an arrest and seizure at the highest possible level in the smuggling organization. Because of Customs' unique search and seizure authority, many of the agency's drug seizures resulted from "cold hits" at or between border points of entry. As a result of this method of operation, Customs (unlike BNDD) rarely went after narcotics suppliers at their foreign sources.

In addition, Customs agents had very little "buy" money with which to purchase evidence and information, as opposed to the large amounts available to BNDD. If Customs agents "bought" drugs, they did so, as one agent put it, "with a badge." Former and current Customs agents claim that because they did not have the authority or resources for a "buy and bust" method of operation, Customs agents spent more of their time developing major conspiracy cases.

But as the new DEA geared up for operation, it adopted none of Customs' strategies and tactics. Instead, it drew the key elements of its organizational structure, its procedures, and its methods largely from BNDD's enforcement program. The DEA's adoption of BNDD's approach was hardly surprising insofar as BNDD personnel constituted approximately 75 per cent of DEA's manpower. Moreover, DEA's mission, though aimed more specifically at apprehending the "principal members of organizations involved in the growing, manufacture, or distribution of controlled substances" and at "reducing the availability of illicit controlled substances on the domestic and international market," was not radically different from BNDD's. Simply put, the objective assigned to DEA in 1973 was "to make cases that penetrate the entire state and international chain which underlies most narcotics transactions, and to uncover those at the highest level who facilitate, organize, and make those transactions possible."[1]

Thus, with the exception of the 700 Customs narcotics agents and support personnel transferred to DEA, the personnel, structure, and strategies of the federal attack on drugs did not change much as a result of Reorganization Plan No. 2. DEA basically proceeded with the core of BNDD's program, and assimilated the transferred Customs agents into the existing BNDD regional structure, where these former Treasury Department employees were instructed to follow the agents' manual previously used in the BNDD organization.

According to interviews with DEA agents who were in the field when Reorganization Plan No. 2 was implemented in July of 1973, the realignment of federal narcotics enforcement activities changed virtually nothing in regional and district offices across the country. One agent summed up the impressions of many others:[2]

> The reorganization was not very traumatic at all. There were small problems in organizing new units in the field but basically we combined easily with Customs agents. I would say the reorganization had virtually no impact at all in the field. For instance, we never did initiate many investigations from interdiction cases and even the addition of Customs personnel did not change this.

The fact that very little changed with the inception of DEA does not mean that the new narcotics agency encountered no difficulties or that it effectively and smoothly carried out the mission charged to it by the architects of Reorganization Plan No. 2. In fact, DEA was troubled in the first years of operation by an assortment of internal and external problems.

Internal Problems

The Leadership Search

The initial problem faced by DEA was finding an effective administrator for the new organization. Because the White House was unable to find the right individual, the new agency was forced to endure a succession of administrators as well as a long period of instability and inconsistency in the top management ranks and a loss of morale among agency members.

John Bartels, the first administrator of DEA, served an undistinguished term lasting less than two years. Bartels was under attack almost from the outset and was never able to assume control of the agency because of a host of internal and external problems. Internally, he had to deal with a demoralized, regionally parochial staff, with infighting among the top-management ranks in Washington, and with personnel integrity problems that soon began to receive a great deal of adverse publicity. Externally, he faced continued hostility from Customs leadership and well-publicized Senate subcommittee hearings on the apparent failure of DEA to have a significant impact in the "war on drugs" despite its broad authority in both foreign and domestic operations.

One former Nixon White House staff member lamented (with the value of hindsight) the appointment of Bartels and assessed the reasons behind the choice in this way:[3]

> *With the choice of Bartels we continued our string of lousy appointments. The one area our Administration was least effective— in fact, we had an abysmal record—was personnel placements. We didn't know the people in law enforcement. We were all lawyers and we were not perceptive to the qualities that make a person a good general manager. The choice of Bartels was a primary reason why DEA had so many problems in carrying out his job.*

Bartels lasted until the middle of 1975; he was succeeded by Peter Bensinger, who was appointed in February of 1976. (Henry Dogin was the acting administrator of the agency in the seven or eight months between the Bartels and Bensinger administrations.) Bensinger was a skillful administrator who steered the DEA to somewhat calmer waters. He did so first by focusing on personnel integrity problems and other divisive issues within the agency, and second, by repairing strained relations between DEA and Congress and between DEA and Customs. However, the early instability caused by the string of executive changes had a decidedly negative impact on the organization, one which undoubtedly affected the performance and achievements of the agency.

Assimilation of Customs Personnel

In addition to enduring the problems brought about by the succession of executive changes, DEA had to deal with the assimilation of Customs agents and support staff into an organization dominated by BNDD personnel. Although Bartels attempted to be fair in the distribution of regional and district posts, he was faced with a no-win situation. Former BNDD employees balked at the assignment of former Customs officers to leadership positions in key regions (such as New York and Miami), and former Customs agents complained about there being "too few" administrative jobs offered them. In the end, approximately one half of the 500 Customs agents who had been transferred to DEA resigned, with a large contingent of these disenchanted agents returning to Customs.[4]

A number of the agents who quit DEA to rejoin Customs defended their actions by attacking the "unsophisticated" methodologies used by DEA (such as the "buy and bust" strategy that Customs narcotics agents derided as far inferior to tactics used by their agency). They also decried what they perceived as DEA's stress on producing arrests and seizures simply for the purpose of generating favorable statistics.

The fact that so many transferred Customs agents returned to the Treasury Department only added to the woes of DEA. The reports these defectors brought back to Customs, including tales of dissension and low morale, reinforced Customs' determination to take the offensive against the stumbling new "lead agency."

External Problems

In addition to coping with these assorted internal problems, DEA had to confront a myriad of unsettling external problems, including the continued hostility of Customs (whose leadership refused to concede anything to DEA without a struggle) and a series of highly critical congressional hearings in which DEA's methodologies came under harsh scrutiny.

Relations with Customs

Even if the character of Customs' reaction on the creation of DEA was not totally unpredictable, the scope and intensity of Customs' obstinance and its reluctance to cooperate was. Several DEA officials who took part in negotiations between the two agencies recalled that several meetings (to which Customs, in the words of one DEA official, was dragged "kicking and screaming") dissolved into shouting matches where little was accomplished.[5] Commissioner Acree of Customs was singled out in particular as a target of DEA's wrath, despite his public posture of support for the reorganization plan. The consensus among DEA officials was that Acree was out to "sabotage" DEA and the reorganization plan. The following comments represent a commonly held view:[6]

> *Acree was very antagonistic, and he and his people tried their best to discredit us by going to the press and to Congress with their problems with us. Although I was transferred to DEA, I still had good friends at Customs and I told them their actions were very unprofessional—and they didn't deny they were trying to screw us. They wanted to make us look bad; we were vulnerable. Customs just couldn't live with losing. As long as they thought the situation was reversible, they were on the attack—at least until Chasen [the new Commissioner of Customs succeeding Acree] came along.*

At first, Customs flooded DEA with leads from narcotics seizure cases that DEA, under its new status, was expected to investigate. However, many of the cases involved small amounts of drugs, such as a few marijuana seeds or joints, and if DEA refused to follow up on the case, Customs would either add that to its compilation of cases DEA refused to respond to or proceed with an investigation of its own. Such tactics infuriated DEA officials, who felt Customs' actions were predicated solely on a desire to embarrass DEA. Indeed, the queasiness felt by DEA may have been justified. Certain Customs officials were later to acknowledge that, beginning in 1973, the Treasury agency believed it could undo the effects of the reorganization by "keeping the fans going" in such a way as to undermine DEA whenever possible. If that meant toying with statistics or racing to place a Customs agent ahead of a DEA official at ports of entry, so be it. The ultimate goal was to see to it that Customs would so rankle and impede DEA that eventually a case could be made to reinvest Customs with the authority it lost in 1973.

However, with the appointment of Robert Chasen as the new Commissioner of Customs in July 1977, relations between DEA and Customs appeared to improve. Chasen seemed committed both to smoothing over past conflicts and to recognizing DEA as the leader in federal narcotics efforts. The assignment of Customs employees to the El Paso Intelligence Center (EPIC), run by DEA, was evidence of Chasen's desire to end the fighting between DEA and his agency. For years Customs had refused to join EPIC because it felt that the new intelligence center should be based in Washington, D.C., rather than in Texas, where DEA believed it would be more beneficial. In addition, Customs' reluctance to assign personnel to EPIC, it was believed, had more to do with Customs' feeling that joining EPIC would be perceived as a capitulation to DEA—that is, as a tacit admission that DEA was, indeed, the lead agency in narcotics enforcement. Chasen's assignment of a Customs contingent to EPIC was considered a positive sign that relations between the two agencies were improving and stabilizing and that perhaps the conflict (detrimental to DEA) was coming to an end.

Yet despite Chasen's apparent commitment to the development of a good working relationship with DEA, interviews with Customs officials indicate that a great deal of hostility still remained within Customs in its attitude toward DEA. According to these individuals, personnel at all levels continued to harbor the belief that one day Customs would regain a major role in drug enforcement. While Chasen did attain a truce of sorts, it was never fully accepted throughout Customs, in part because Chasen himself was not well liked or trusted by long-time Customs personnel.

Relations with Congress

Coping with the problems brought about by hostile relations with a rival organization was not the only external threat encountered by DEA. On top of the frustration of the continuing interagency battle came a series of hard-hitting congressional hearings (held by the Permanent Subcommittee on Investigations, chaired by Senator Henry M. Jackson).

The hearings commenced on June 9, 1975, with months of

committee staff investigations preceding the public sessions. They were triggered primarily by a Justice Department investigation, authorized by Attorney General Edward H. Levi, into alleged irregularities and mismanagement in DEA. Complicating the entire matter was the dismissal of the first administrator of DEA, John Bartels, on May 30, 1975, eleven days before the start of the committee hearings. The hearings culminated in an interim committee report accusing DEA of an abysmally inadequate performance that could not be blamed on the lack of cooperation of other agencies.[7]

The Jackson hearings addressed a number of issues, principally the methodologies used by DEA, the makeup and interaction of federal agencies involved in drug enforcement, and the dominant political issue—personnel integrity within the agency. Perhaps the most important findings presented in the subcommittee report were those critical of the strategies and methodologies employed by DEA. The sharpest criticism was reserved for DEA's large expenditures of money for the purchase of information and evidence, a strategy DEA employed in the hope that it would permit agents to infiltrate the top hierarchy of major drug trafficking rings. The subcommittee also suggested that DEA's virtually exclusive undercover work not only helped to account for the agency's poor performance record but also was a cause of the agency's integrity problems since undercover work exposes agents to potential corruption.[8]

DEA personnel considered the congressional proceedings unwarranted, biased, and detrimental to the image and morale of the agency. Lower-level officials in DEA were especially bitter over what they felt was the reluctance of the Justice Department to allow DEA to return the fire directed at them. As one DEA agent explained:[9]

> *[Senator] Jackson was trying to pull us apart and the department didn't want us to fight them. During those proceedings it was like an armed camp around here; nobody knew what was going to happen next. And Jackson really creamed us, he really did a job on this agency. His committee brought things up which had been thoroughly investigated and reinvestigated. Given what we went through, given our morale at the time, it's a wonder we continued to function, that we even exist today.*

Regardless of whether the work of the Jackson committee had merit, the fact remains that the congressional hearings were perceived within DEA as another attack, one that had to be faced and responded to, and at great cost to the morale and performance of the agency.

Prospects of Another Reorganization

Perhaps the most serious external threat to DEA came in 1981 in the form of new calls for another reorganization of federal narcotics activities and jurisdictions. Rumors of a possible further realignment of federal drug agencies first flared up publicly in the early summer of 1981 and were fanned in July when Peter Bensinger, the head of DEA, was removed from his post by the Reagan Administration. The reasons for Bensinger's dismissal were clear: The Administration was dismayed by the Justice Department's assessment that DEA was losing the war on drugs, disturbed by reports of Bensinger's failure to act the part of the "loyal team player" (he had lobbied in Congress against budget cuts the Administration wanted to make in DEA), and concerned about Bensinger's unenthusiastic reaction to a preliminary Administration proposal to merge DEA with the FBI.[10]

Accompanying the official confirmation of Bensinger's resignation were reports that Reagan Administration officials were seriously considering a reorganization that would result in an assimilation by the FBI of most of DEA's personnel and tasks. The appointment of Francis M. Mullen, Jr., the executive assistant director of the FBI, as acting head of DEA served to enhance the belief of many in the drug law enforcement community that such a merger lay in the future for DEA.

Bensinger, in a news conference announcing his resignation, alluded to the potential DEA-FBI merger by noting that while a close relationship with the FBI would be welcomed by DEA, neither he nor others within DEA were convinced that a realignment would produce better results in the effort to stem the flow of illicit narcotics.[11] Although a consolidation of the two agencies was by no means a foregone conclusion, comments by Bensinger and Justice Department officials in mid-1981 clearly indicated that the Reagan Administration was eager to add the FBI's assets to the federal attack on drugs and had formed a study group to review various options that would accomplish this goal.

The Reagan Administration's eventual decision (in January,

1982) to have DEA join forces with the FBI was not a new idea.[12] In fact, suggestions to hand the FBI a major role in federal narcotics law enforcement activities date to J. Edgar Hoover's tenure as director of the FBI. However, it was Hoover's view—one shared by almost all within the FBI—that drug activities were a nontraditional, "dirty" business with great potential for the corruption of agents working undercover. As a result, top leadership in the FBI had repeatedly resisted and declined the addition of narcotics duties to the agency's existing array of responsibilities. Hoover and others were convinced that any benefits of accepting drug enforcement tasks would be more than offset by the risk of tarnishing the Bureau's reputation and strict standards of behavior if FBI agents were exposed to the temptations inherent in undercover narcotics activities.

Indeed, the reluctance of the FBI to augment its role with drug enforcement activities was one major reason why the 1973 reorganization task force rejected the option of transferring narcotics functions and authority to the FBI. Roy Ash, among others, worried at the time that even if the FBI could be persuaded to accept narcotics tasks, a "potentially serious disruption and a loss of momentum in drug enforcement" might occur owing to the "lack of FBI experience with drugs and the magnitude of necessary organizational transfers."[13]

Given the past history of the FBI's attitude toward drug enforcement, an important question deserves attention: how successful will a consolidation be, given the nature of the tasks in each organization—tasks that differ in fundamental ways.

While top officials in both the Justice Department and the White House stopped short of an official merger between DEA and the FBI, such a formal consolidation remains a possibility. At present, however, DEA will retain its existing structure, personnel, and management, a move palatable to both DEA and the FBI; Associate Attorney General Rudolph W. Giuliani has argued that such a move would bring all the benefits of a formal merger, but none of the costs or drawbacks.[14]

The willingness of FBI and Justice Department officials to accept a role long disdained may be tied to the nature of investigations conducted by the FBI in recent years. The well-publicized ABSCAM operation, as well as other investigations into organized crime, political corruption, and probes of major drug cartels, all have underlined the Bureau's increased acceptance of undercover tactics—techniques that are in some ways similar, though not identical to, those used by narcotics agents in DEA.

Many observers believe that the FBI has much to offer the lagging federal effort against drug traffickers: greater clout with state and local officials and the State Department, greater resources in terms of personnel and funding levels, and the greater experience of the largest law enforcement agency in making inroads into organized crime.

Other observers are far less sanguine about the gains to be reaped by such a formal merger of the two organizations. Peter Bensinger and Senator Sam Nunn (D.–Ga.) both have pointed out that recent reorganizations of narcotics agencies have resulted in initial declines in arrests and seizures and reductions in the overall general effectiveness of the federal drug enforcement effort.[15] More specific concerns have centered on (1) the limited experience of the FBI with operations overseas and possible reluctance of foreign governments to deal with our domestic intelligence agency and (2) opposition of state and local law enforcement officers to the proposed merger.[16]

Perhaps the most important reservation about folding DEA into the FBI focuses on the risk of creating much upheaval for no significant gain and on the sheer difficulty of merging two organizations with decidedly different methods of operation. For example, Robert Van Etten, national president of the Federal Law Enforcement Officers Association, suggests that yet another reorganization might not address the fundamental causes of DEA's failure to show marked progress in the war cn drugs. To Van Etten and others, significant improvements in efficiency and effectiveness will occur only through increased attention to the system used for measuring the success of narcotics enforcement activities, and through increased attention to the entire federal drug enforcement philosophy guiding federal activities in this arena.[17] Without a reassessment of the procedures and tactics currently in use, a formal merger of the DEA and the FBI might result in nothing more than a disruptive reshuffling and a lowering of morale (not uncommon consequences of reorganizations).

Summary

The Drug Enforcement Administration failed to meet the expectations of its architects not because of faulty organizational structure or design, but rather because the basic drug enforcement methods and strategies it employed were no different from those used by the agencies that preceded DEA. The reorganization produced no fundamental change because those who planned it failed to go beyond a mere reshuffling of personnel and formal lines of jurisdiction to ascertain how the actual behavior of agents might or might not be affected by the reorganization. For DEA to have succeeded, it would have had to make fundamental changes in its style of operation. Instead, DEA merely continued with the same personnel (with the exception of 700 Customs agents and support personnel, all of whom had little effect on DEA), the same management, and the same operating styles of BNDD.[18] As a result, interagency conflicts persisted, and the development of major conspiracy cases remained unsatisfactory.

The results of the 1973 reorganization will be even more disappointing if policymakers ignore the principal lesson of this experience: Serious questions need to be explored before any further reorganization (such as a politically expedient merger of DEA with the FBI) is undertaken. As James Q. Wilson has suggested, without a careful, detailed examination of the operating level tasks (and the resources essential to their performance), we cannot know whether the FBI and the DEA are even compatible. It is essential to know, for example, (1) whether the agents in both organizations are engaged in similar tasks, (2) whether the operations employ "similar resources in similar ways," and (3) whether tactics and resources found useful in one organization would necessarily be useful or appropriate in the other.[19] In the absence of this kind of knowledge, any future mergers would likely be no more successful than the many narcotics enforcement reorganizations of the past. For without a serious effort to rethink and redirect the federal attack on drugs, no reorganization will succeed in altering in a substantive way federal drug law enforcement. The reorganization of 1973 proved that.

Endnotes

1. U.S., Congress, Senate, Committee on Government Operations, *Federal Drug Enforcement, Hearings before the Permanent Subcommittee on Investigations of the Senate Committee on Government Operations*, 94th Cong., 2d sess., 1976, part 5, p. 1359.
2. Interview with DEA narcotics agents, May 1978.
3. Interview with former Nixon White House staff member, February 1978.
4. Interviews with DEA officials, May 1978.
5. Interviews with DEA officials, May 1978.
6. Interview with DEA official, May 1978.
7. U.S. Congress, Senate, Committee on Government Operations, *Federal Narcotics Enforcement, Interim Report of the Permanent Subcommittee on Investigations of the Senate Committee on Government Operations*, S. Rept. 94–1039, 94th Cong., 2d sess., 1976, p. 182.
8. *Ibid.*, pp. 44, 46.
9. Interview with DEA official, May 1978.
10. *The New York Times*, 17 June 1981, p. A 18; and *The Washington Post*, 13 June 1981, p. A 9. In addition, interviews with Justice Department officials confirmed that these were the primary factors involved in the decision to ask for Bensinger's resignation.
11. *The New York Times*, 17 June 1981, p. A 18.
12. *The New York Times*, 12 June 1981, p. 1.
13. Memorandum from Roy Ash to President Richard Nixon, "Drug Enforcement Reorganization," p. 6. Of additional concern was Ash's fear that congressional questioning over a transfer of narcotics tasks to the FBI might blossom into a major issue in the upcoming hearings on the appointment of L. Patrick Gray to head the FBI, and could have an adverse impact on Gray's chances.
14. *The New York Times*, 12 June 1981, p. 1.
15. *Ibid.*, p. 17.
16. *Ibid.*
17. *The New York Times*, 8 August 1981, p. 20.
18. Mark M. Moore, "Reorganization Plan #2 Reviewed: Problems in Implementing a Strategy to Reduce the Supply of Drugs to Illicit Markets in the United States," *Public Policy* 26 (Spring 1978):249.
19. James Q. Wilson, *The Investigators* (New York: Basic Books, 1978), pp. 211–13.

Chapter 10

CONCLUSIONS

If students of federal reorganization agree on anything, it is that few reorganizations are successful in achieving fully the results desired and promised by their architects. Least successful, as both Frederick Mosher and Anthony Downs have pointed out, are those reorganizations aimed at influencing or altering the behavior of lower-level operators in an agency and those meant to produce programmatic changes.[1] Downs is especially critical of reorganizations that are generated by top-level officials and are expected to penetrate down to those employees who actually carry out the tasks of the organization. Such reorganizations, he suggests, are rarely meaningful or successful and may stimulate nothing more than another call for reorganization.[2] And this is no small part of the problem. As Rufus Miles has commented, "Repetitive reorganization without proper initial diagnosis is like repetitive surgery without proper diagnosis: obviously an unsound and unhealthy approach to the cure of the malady."[3]

The federal narcotics law enforcement arena provides a case in point. The organizational landscape was dramatically altered in 1968. But the organizational problems proved stubborn, so the Nixon Administration proposed Reorganization Plan No. 2 in 1973. It was a serious, well-intentioned effort to reorganize narcotics agency jurisdictions. But it resulted neither in dramatic improvements in the reduction and control of illicit drug trafficking nor in any radical change in the methods and strategies by which federal narcotics enforcement agencies seek to accomplish their goals. Instead, the reorganization led to a series of unintended and unanticipated consequences such as continued clashes between

145

the relevant agencies. And by 1981 the failures had given rise to yet another call for reorganization of federal narcotics activities.

Experience suggests that the failure of the Nixon Administration to fashion an effective reorganization in this area—that is, one with a substantive impact on federal narcotics activities—is not an unusual outcome of reorganizations. Certainly Nixon's predecessors and most of his successors have encountered similar experiences, where reorganization has led more to disappointment and disillusionment than to fulfillment and noticeable improvements.

Reorganization Failures

The scholarly literature on federal executive reorganization acknowledges that it is the rare reorganization that has a substantial impact on the output of affected agencies or on the delivery of public services. And a wide array of explanations have been offered to account for these consistent failures and dashed expectations. Among the more prominent explanations are the following:

1. Not every reorganization is in fact a serious, substantive effort to affect the efficiency and effectiveness of agency activities. Some reorganizations, after all, are intended to be merely symbolic, elevating or lowering the organizational status of an agency to indicate an alteration in the priority attached to its functions. Some reorganizations are intended to be merely cosmetic, offering the *appearance* of action or change. That is, carrying out a major reorganization can be a way for a president to appear to be "doing something" about a problem—to seem to be taking bold and decisive action. Finally, a reorganization can be based on much more specific political motives, such as fulfillment of a campaign promise or the movement of particular individuals into or out of certain positions.[4]

2. Even reorganizations seemingly intended to affect organizational output are often too superficial in nature, focusing more on the *theoretical* lines of authority and jurisdiction than on anything else.[5] Architects of reorganizations seem to get their notions (or at least their rationales) from some formulary of organizational management principles that have little relation to actual

behavior inside real organizations. It is not surprising, then, that perfunctory reorganizations based on familiar nostrums and maxims will have little substantive effect.

3. Reorganizations often appear to be failures because we expect too much too soon.[6] The problem here is that reorganization is mistakenly perceived as a single *event* rather than a slow *process*, and that misperception leads to disappointment when the intended results are not immediately forthcoming and visible. This problem is exacerbated by the unfortunate tendency of executives to try yet another organizational setup before the dust has settled from the last reshuffling. It is little wonder that some agencies yield unimpressive results when they are constantly subjected to disruptive reorganizations.

4. The architects of reorganizations often *draft* their plans in political vacuums, viewing the restructuring as solely an organizational or managerial problem unattended by political considerations and implications.[7] In view of this absurdity, it is no wonder that reorganizers typically encounter more serious opposition than they expect at the proposal stage, or that reorganizations, once implemented, are fraught with unanticipated and untoward consequences.

5. The architects of reorganizations often do their work in secret, rejecting the participation of persons in the organizations to be affected. This secrecy is maintained in an effort to minimize the opposition of employees or constituent groups that have a vested interest in preserving the status quo.[8] It is a practice, however, that has clear drawbacks because it precludes input by persons knowledgeable about the tasks and routines, familiar with the political and organizational landscapes, and capable of foreseeing potential consequences of certain courses of action.

There is much truth in each of these explanations. It is easy to point to one or another of them as the principal cause for any particular reorganization's failure. The problem here is that, although the general literature offers numerous theories to explain the deficiencies and failures of executive reorganizations, very few case studies are available to test such theories. Worse yet, almost no attention has been paid in the scholarly literature to the *consequences* of reorganization to judge whether these plans have actually achieved the intent of their architects—and if not, why not.[9]

Thus, the narcotics enforcement case study presented here is useful and instructive in at least two respects. First, it helps to fill the empirical void in the literature by going beyond a routine analysis of the politics and process of reorganization and examines in detail the implementation of a plan and its ensuing consequences (both intended and unintended). Second, the case is instructive because, with the value of hindsight, it is possible to see what kind of analysis would have been necessary for the architects of Reorganization Plan No. 2 to improve federal narcotics law enforcement. This, in turn, provides an empirical basis from which to generate a better explanation for the frequent failure of reorganizations to make any real difference in the way federal agencies behave.

Reorganization Plan No. 2: The Unasked Questions

The failure of the Drug Enforcement Administration to meet the expectations of its architects raises questions that are substantive and important. Given the disappointing results of the reorganization, were there any other kinds of analysis or other methods of research that could have generated relevant information affecting the eventual design and probable outcomes of the reorganization? Were the desired improvements feasible given the statutory authority of those federal agencies involved in narcotics enforcement activities? Was there any way to determine in advance what difficulties were likely to emerge once implementation of the plan began?

Interviews with key officials involved in drafting the reorganization reveal that although the committee had at its disposal performance data summaries for five agencies with narcotics-related activities (BNDD, INS, and ODALE in the Justice Department; the Customs Service and the IRS in the Treasury Department), the committee did not use these data in drawing up the reorganization options. The tendency of the reorganization task force to disregard statistics that might have been useful in gauging an agency's effectiveness was reflected throughout the group's investigation. The task force basically limited itself to a review of the legal jurisdictions, agency reputations, and the previous narcotics backgrounds of the organizations selected for restructuring.

At no point did anyone suggest or undertake a comprehensive review of the probable impact of the proposed alternatives on the agents in the field. In fact, no field studies whatsoever were conducted during the long process of creating the plan. It was not until after submission of the plan to Congress and not until congressional members requested relevant facts and figures that OMB officials sent staff members into the field to collect information on the probable effects of the reorganization.

The principal problem with the nature of the task force's research, however, was the lack of analysis on the comparative effectiveness of the different strategies employed in drug law enforcement activities. The reorganization task force never studied the methods employed by BNDD, Customs, or ODALE—the principal units affected by the reorganization.

Neither the architects of the reorganization nor any of their staff members tried to measure the effectiveness of the strategies then in use or to offer suitable replacements for them. In short, the planners failed (and thus the reorganization failed) to address important and fundamental questions: (1) whether the "buy and bust" strategy used by the old BNDD and adopted by DEA is a good or bad strategy; (2) whether conspiracy cases are worth the large, long-term commitment of resources; (3) whether the waste incurred by the use of funds to purchase evidence and information is avoidable or simply inherent in the nature of narcotics law enforcement; and (4) whether the emphasis on lower-level arrests and seizures was the wrong approach for whatever reasons. Neither the reorganization plan itself nor the analysis that preceded it raised in any serious or substantive way questions about *what* DEA was supposed to do and *how* it might go about doing it.

Thus, not surprisingly DEA ended up adopting the strategies and tactics used by the old BNDD; after all, former BNDD personnel accounted for 75 per cent of DEA's work force. Yet it is precisely because of DEA's emphasis on a "buy and bust" strategy (and its consequent failure to convict a large number of high-level traffickers through the development of conspiracy cases) that the agency came under criticism from Congress, OMB, and other governmental units. It also helps to explain the charge that the reorganization failed. Had those in charge of creating the reorganization tried to think through the nature of the enforcement task, perhaps the reorganization plan could have been designed in a way that would have altered drastically the output of the organizations involved.

In order to affect the output of the new agency, staff members would have had to produce more empirical research by studying front-line operators who were performing tasks in a specific way and to ask how the tasks could be changed and with what effect. They might have explored, for example, whether it was possible to build conspiracy cases implicating high-echelon drug traffickers without a continuing stress on street-level, undercover activities and the accompanying lower-level arrests and seizures. Or was the conspiracy strategy in fact inextricably bound up in a "buy and bust" strategy, dependent on the infiltration of undercover agents into the lower echelons of major drug smuggling organizations?

The reorganization task force's performance of the type of analysis outlined above would have required a large and skilled staff with enough time to conduct research in the field as well as in the agencies' headquarters in Washington. Although putting together a staff of sufficient size and skill to produce an intensive and thorough study of drug law enforcement activities was undoubtedly possible, finding the time to do so was another matter. The decision to reorganize drug enforcement activities stemmed from a perceived crisis, in which agency competition and conflict were thought to be having debilitating effects on the Administration's "war on drugs." This, coupled with such other factors as the upcoming expiration of the president's reorganization authority and the preparation of narcotics reorganization plans by others in the federal government, served to narrow the time frame in which a reorganization plan could be developed.

As a result, the creation of Reorganization Plan No. 2 was basically a top-down, generalist operation, with the participation by the agencies to be affected limited only to persons at the highest executive levels. Because the kind of analyses described here were not conducted, the final reorganization proposal was unable to do that which it was later attacked for failing to do: produce marked improvement in the federal narcotics enforcement effort.

Not surprisingly, then, little changed with the reorganization's implementation. The basics of the federal attack on drugs did not change because no one *tried* to change them. No one charged

with the development of structural changes in federal drug activities went into the field to determine how the behavior of field
agents might or might not be affected by the reorganization.
Rather, it was assumed that by altering the general organizational
structure of the federal effort, the result would be a more efficient
and effective delivery of an important public service. Apparently
no one, at the time the reorganization plan was being drafted,
appreciated that operational changes would be necessary to
produce a significant change in the behavior of a new lead agency
in narcotics. And no one, it seems, stopped to consider if such
changes could even be achieved.[10]

The Proper Analysis

The kind of analysis necessary, then, to produce significant, substantive changes requires not the usual top-down analysis typically
used by reorganization task forces, but rather an analytical approach that focuses on the behavior of those persons who perform
the tasks basic to the organization's mission—for example, the
forest ranger, the Internal Revenue Service auditor, the Wage
and Hour Division compliance officer, the OSHA inspector, the
DEA narcotics agent. The Carter Administration, for example,
seemed to take a step in this direction when the President's Reorganization Project (PRP) announced the adoption of what
it considered an innovative "bottom-up" approach to executive
reorganization that sought to identify problems of service delivery
by inviting citizens to submit comments on perceived agency
problems.[11]

Although the PRP was correct in beginning its analysis at the
bottom of the organization, it soon discovered that asking citizens
for comments was not the right approach. What *was* necessary
were examinations in both field offices and agency headquarters
of tasks and procedures. In order to draw up a reorganization plan
that will produce a major change in the output of a federal agency
(or agencies), the reorganization architects must understand
clearly the tasks of the agency's front-line employees and must
discern what modifications in their tasks would be necessary to
produce the intended changes in the agency's behavior. For if
after the reorganization those front-line employees continue to

perform their service delivery task in the same way, whatever other changes are produced by the reorganization will be of little consequence. But such analysis necessarily involves much more than the Carter task force's perfunctory solicitation of comments from citizens. Rather, it requires that reorganization planners conduct carefully detailed examinations of the target agency's basic tasks and procedures—in field offices as well as at agency headquarters. Without conducting such studies, the chance of producing a meaningful alteration or improvement in the output of an organization will be poor.

The Elusive Formula for Successful Reorganization

The kind of analysis described above, necessary to produce reorganizations that result in serious, substantive change, is rarely, if ever, performed by reorganization task forces assembled by the White House. The reason—and there should be no misunderstanding on this point—is not that reorganization planners are incompetent or lacking in public administration skills. Rather, this kind of analysis is usually not undertaken because of a variety of cognitive and political constraints. For example, it may not always be easy to conceive of new ways of performing a certain task. Similarly, it may not always be clear what the consequences would be of changes in the way front-line employees carry out their tasks. More important, however, are the extraordinary political obstacles inherent in the nature of reorganization efforts.

First, to overcome the inertia of a political system that tends to resist change, presidents must be willing to expend a large amount of political capital. Since the president's reservoir of political capital is not infinite, judicious decisions must be made about how much to spend in pursuit of any particular reorganization goal. Moreover, a president who is willing to spend some of that capital must be able to convince others that the objective is worthwhile. This carries the obvious disadvantage of leading to unrealistic expectations for a reorganization's results. The president, in an effort to sell the reorganization plan to the public and to skeptical bureaucrats and legislators, will promise dramatic results and will raise hopes that may be impossible to meet. The history of executive branch reorganization is replete with examples that fit this pattern. For instance, the 1970 proposal to reorganize the U.S. Postal Service was accompanied by a well-organized campaign intended to "sell" the reorganization plan to the general public, Congress, and various special interest groups. As John T. Tierney has noted:[12]

> *The reorganization's proponents unabashedly claimed that the new organization would cut costs, improve services, and remove the postal deficit. . . . In short, there was a rhetorical spiral at work in the period before and immediately following the re-organization, pushing expectations well beyond what was likely under even the best conditions.*

In short, a president's effort to win a reorganization in which a fair amount of political capital has been invested may lead to inflated and unrealistic expectations.

Second, to convince others that a major reorganization is justified, a president may need some natural advantages, such as a crisis or a scandal. If one succeeds in showing that a crisis exists, however, there will be a need to move quickly to demonstrate that one is in control of the situation. Yet this conflicts with the need to spend the time necessary to study thoroughly those units being reorganized.

Third, it is much easier and safer for reorganizers to avoid recommendations for specific changes in agency operations and to build their case instead on traditional reorganization proverbs. To do so is to lessen the risk of alienating people who might balk at suggestions for a reorganization aimed at altering agency behavior. For example, Congress has always proved to be a tough obstacle to presidential reorganization. Congressional committees are leery of approving any reorganization that would radically alter the traditional lines of jurisdiction and authority within the legislative body. The opposition of powerful "subsystems" can itself be sufficient to frustrate the most carefully laid plans for reorganization. And congressional committees would be as perturbed (if not more) over reorganization plans that may contain controversial alterations in tasks; committee members can be expected to react negatively to reorganization plans that seem to entail hidden policy changes. Fourth, the more time spent doing the proper kinds of analysis, the more resistance reorganizers would be bound to encounter, and the more opportunities there would be for adversaries to mobilize the opposition.

This all helps to explain why reorganizations are top-down, generalist operations, employed as a response to crisis, scandal, mismanagement, or a renewed national commitment. It helps to explain why we rarely, if ever, see a reorganization proposal based on a thorough and detailed analysis of agencies' tasks and procedures: it is politically infeasible to do so.

Given all this, no one should be surprised when what the government is doing after a reorganization is not substantially different from what it was doing before the reorganization. In the plain language of former director of the OMB James T. Lynn: "It doesn't do any good to take garbage out of an old can and put it in a new can. It'll stink just as much."[13] If the same people are doing the same thing in the same way—though perhaps in a different location—there will be no operational change. We should not be surprised, then, when allegedly serious, well-intentioned reorganizations, such as the 1973 restructuring of federal narcotics activities, do not live up to advanced billings or result in a dramatic increase in the effectiveness of governmental actions.

Improving the Chances for Success

The preceding discussion is not to suggest that the tool of reorganization serves no useful purpose or that a reorganization never satisfies the desires of its architects. Reorganizations may prove useful, for example, if only (1) to provide a semblance of action, (2) to respond to outside pressures for immediate, tangible solutions to well-publicized organizational problems, (3) as a convenient way to move persons into or out of power, or (4) as a means of "shaking up" an entrenched bureaucracy.[14]

Moreover, as many students of federal reorganization have observed, reorganizations often seek to serve "a host of different purposes, often at the same time."[15] But these same scholars and practitioners note that two of the most common and important types of reorganizations—those whose goals focus on economy and efficiency and those with goals aimed at increased policy effectiveness—are the most difficult to accomplish. Lester Salamon, for example, suggests that the very difficulty of convincing the natural opponents of reorganization (most notably, Congress and federal agencies) of its potential benefits can encourage a "conspiracy of silence about the real goals of reorganization." As a result, reorganizers may eschew the most important and relevant arguments favoring their proposals and advance the plans instead on grounds that are "largely specious."[16]

One might conclude, then, as have Salamon and others, that the conventional principles advanced with reorganizations are flawed to the point where they become a straitjacket making the serious, substantive goals of reorganization—at the least—more difficult to achieve.[17] For example, Harold Seidman has likened the skills necessary for justifying reorganization proposals as more akin to those of a "Talmudic scholar than to those of a sophisticated political scientist."[18]

Is reorganization, weighted as it is under the traditional principles, a futile exercise like "trying to make water run uphill," as John Ehrlichman once phrased it?[19] Is reorganization so costly and so disruptive that it is best seen as a pathological practice of governmental management? This is, to be sure, a rather dim view, but an understandable one. For executive reorganization to result in a more effective and rational functioning of the federal government, we need to rethink the different rationales on which reorganizations are predicated, paying more attention to the kind of reorganization that will result in serious, substantive change and to how the established principles of reorganization may be altered to reflect such goals.

This task does not promise to be easy; perhaps it is an impossible one. Changing the methods of research employed by reorganization planners might help. Altering the accompanying rationales or justifications to reflect output-related concerns might also help. But to do so would require the scaling of some rather formidable political barriers. However, with changed principles, chances are better that goals can be more openly articulated and the desired ends more clearly expressed. This in turn may assuage the fears of traditional opponents to reorganizations, affording presidents a chance to seek effective change through an effective medium.

Endnotes

1. Frederick C. Mosher, *Governmental Reorganizations* (Indianapolis: The Bobbs-Merrill Co., 1967), p. 514; and Anthony Downs, *Inside Bureaucracy* (Boston: Little, Brown & Co., 1967), p. 166.

2. Downs, *Inside Bureaucracy*, pp. 165–66.

3. Rufus E. Miles, Jr., "Considerations for a President Bent on Reorganization," *Public Administration Review* 37 (March/April 1977):160.

4. See George D. Greenberg, "Reorganization Reconsidered: The U.S. Public Health Service 1960–1973," *Public Policy* 23 (Fall 1975):483–86; Harold Seidman, *Politics, Position, and Power*, 3d ed. (New York: Oxford University Press, 1980), pp. 24–25; and Herbert Emmerich, *Federal Organization and Administrative Management* (University: University of Alabama Press, 1971), pp. 155, 157–58.

5. See David S. Brown, "Reforming the Bureaucracy: Some Suggestions for the New President," *Public Administration Review* 37 (March/April 1977); and Tyrus G. Fain, ed., *Federal Reorganization: The Executive Branch* (New York: R. R. Bowker Co., 1977), p. x.

6. See Fain, *Federal Reorganization* and Emmerich, *Federal Organization and Administrative Management*, pp. 7–8.

7. See John R. Dempsey, "Carter Reorganization: A Midterm Appraisal," *Public Administration Review* 39 (January/February, 1979):75; Peri E. Arnold, "Reorganization and Politics: A Reflection on the Adequacy of Administrative Theory," *Public Administration Review* 34 (May/June 1974):205–11; Seidman, *Politics, Position, and Power*, p. 14; and Fain, *Federal Reorganization*, p. x.

8. See Brown, "Reforming the Bureaucracy;" Douglas M. Fox, "The President's Proposals for Executive Reorganization: A Critique," *Public Administration Review* 33 (September/October 1973):404; and Mosher, *Governmental Reorganizations*, pp. 306–58.

9. The dearth of empirical literature focusing on exactly what reorganizations do accomplish has been noted by many, including Douglas M. Fox, *Managing the Public's Interest* (New York: Holt, Rinehart and Winston, 1979), p. 63; Harold Seidman in "A Mini-Symposium: President Nixon's Proposals for Executive Reorganization," Douglas M. Fox, ed., *Public Administration Review* 34 (September/October 1974): 489; and Lester M. Salamon, "The Goals of Reorganization," *Administration and Society* 12 (February 1981):474.

10. Had the right questions been asked, had the proper street-level studies been conducted, possibly those charged with developing a reorganization plan would have concluded that the nature of the problem could not be affected by changing the structure of the federal narcotics effort, by establishing a "lead" agency in narcotics. Given the nature of Customs' mission and tasks, one can never completely remove that agency from a role in the federal narcotics attack, primarily because of its statutory need and authority to maintain a border presence. Yet it is understandable why many were convinced that the proper place for narcotics law enforcement activities was in the Justice Department—a location in which such functions seem logically to belong.

11. Seidman, *Politics, Position, and Power*, 2d ed., p. 127.

12. John T. Tierney, *Postal Reorganization, Managing the Public's Business* (Boston: Auburn House Publishing Co., 1981), p. 175.

13. Douglas M. Fox, *Managing the Public's Interest*, p. 68.
14. Seidman, *Politics, Position, and Power*, 2d ed., pp. 24–25.
15. Salamon, "The Goals of Reorganization," p. 478.
16. *Ibid.,* p. 493.
17. See, for example, Fox, *Managing the Public's Interest*, p. 77; Salamon, "The Goals of Reorganization," p. 498; and Seidman, *Politics, Position, and Power*, pp. 10–15.
18. Seidman, *Politics, Position, and Power*, p. 10.
19. Fox, *Managing the Public's Interest*, p. 48.

INDEX